W9-BLU-969

A hand to hold, an opinion to reject

Other Cathy Books From Andrews, McMeel & Parker

Thin thighs in thirty years
Wake me up when I'm a size 5
Men should come with instruction booklets
A mouthful of breath mints and no one to kiss
Another Saturday night of wild and reckless abandon
Eat your way to a better relationship

A hand to hold, an opinion to reject

A cathy® Collection

by Cathy Guisewite

Andrews, McMeel & Parker
A Universal Press Syndicate Affiliate
Kansas City • New York

Cathy® is syndicated internationally by Universal Press Syndicate.

A hand to hold, an opinion to reject © 1987 by Universal Press Syndicate. All rights reserved. Printed in the United States of America. No part of this book may be used or reproduced in any manner whatsoever without permission except in the case of reprints in the context of reviews. For information write Andrews, McMeel & Parker, a Universal Press Syndicate Affiliate, 4900 Main Street, Kansas City, Missouri 64112.
ISBN: 0-8362-2092-7
Library of Congress Catalog Card Number: 87-71164

ATTENTION: SCHOOLS AND BUSINESSES

Andrews, McMeel & Parker books are available at quantity discounts with bulk purchase for educational, business, or sales promotional use. For information, please write to: Special Sales Department, Andrews, McMeel & Parker, 4900 Main Street, Kansas City, Missouri 64112.

I WON'T SPEND AN EVENING WITH A GUY UNLESS HE HAS REAL POTENTIAL.
I WON'T SPEND AN HOUR!
IF A GUY DOESN'T SHOW PROMISE, I WON'T GIVE HIM 10 MINUTES!
LIFE'S TOO SHORT! DAYS ARE TOO PRECIOUS!
WE DON'T HAVE TIME TO WASTE ON THE WRONG GUY !!!
...WE'RE TOO BUSY WASTING IT WITH OUR GIRLFRIENDS.

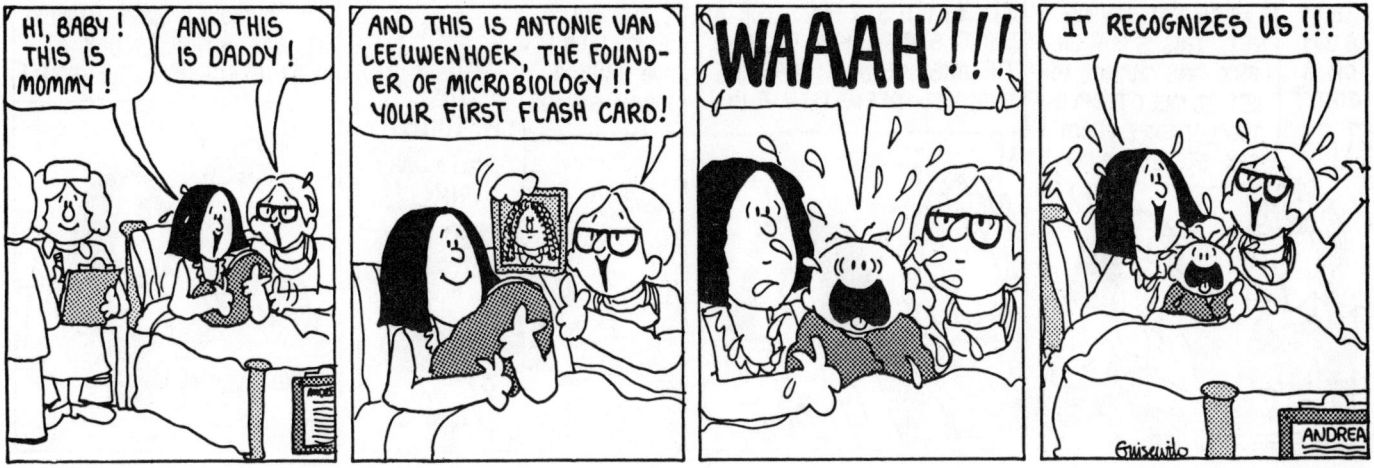
HI, BABY! THIS IS MOMMY!
AND THIS IS DADDY!
AND THIS IS ANTONIE VAN LEEUWENHOEK, THE FOUNDER OF MICROBIOLOGY!! YOUR FIRST FLASH CARD!
WAAAH!!!
IT RECOGNIZES US!!!
ANDREA

ANDREA AND I HAVE GREAT RESPECT FOR NATURAL HUMAN INSTINCTS.
WE WANT OUR STAY HERE TO BE AS EASY, UNCOMPLICATED AND BRIEF AS POSSIBLE.
WE'RE HEALTHY, HAPPY, RESPONSIBLE, AND ASK FOR NOTHING EXCEPT A LITTLE QUIET TIME TOGETHER.
MORE TROUBLEMAKERS.
21

UNISEX CLOTHES... UNISEX COLORS... UNISEX TOYS...
UNISEX BLANKETS... UNISEX BOOKS... UNISEX MOBILES... UNISEX BOOTIES...
cat
OH, WHAT A CUTE LITTLE..UH....UH.....
WHAT DO YOU MEAN YOU CAN'T TELL IF IT'S A BOY OR A GIRL?!
BABY NURSE

IS IT A BOY OR A GIRL?
WE'RE NOT SAYING YET. THIS IS OUR BABY'S ONE CHANCE TO GET TO MEET PEOPLE TOTALLY FREE FROM SEX STEREOTYPING.

I'LL BET IT'S A BOY...LOOK AT THAT STRONG FIST!...AND THE MISCHIEVOUS SPARKLE. ...OH, YES. DEFINITELY A BOY.

...AND WHAT A KICKER! YOU HAVE A TOUGH, STRONG.
GIRL! SHE'S A GIRL! A TOUGH, STRONG GIRL!!

OH, I SHOULD HAVE KNOWN IT WAS A GIRL! LOOK AT THAT PRECIOUS LITTLE DIMPLE.
NURSES STATION #2

THE STATUE OF LIBERTY...
LIFE

PEOPLE WORSHIP HER...PHOTOGRAPH HER...WRITE SONGS TO HER...AND TRAVEL FROM THE ENDS OF THE EARTH JUST FOR A GLIMPSE OF HER!

WHY CAN THIS WOMAN STILL INSPIRE THE SAME PASSION AT AGE 100??!
LIFE

BECAUSE SHE'S FRENCH.
PASS THE NACHOS.

YOU'RE NOT STILL IN BED, ARE YOU, CATHY?
BED? ARE YOU KIDDING, MOM?! IT'S NOON!

THIS IS OUR ONLY LONG WEEKEND ALL SUMMER! I WOULDN'T THINK OF WASTING IT IN BED!!

BED! I THOUGHT YOU KNEW ME BETTER THAN THAT! BED! HA, HA!! THAT'S A GOOD ONE!!

SNORE
CLUNK.

WE'RE CALLING HER "ZENITH", CATHY.
"ZENITH"?
"ZENITH": THE PEAK! THE BEST! THE ULTIMATE! THE PINNACLE OF EXCELLENCE!
IT'S A NAME THAT SUMS UP THE VISION UPON WHICH OUR WHOLE GENERATION WAS FOUNDED!
"ZENITH": THE TV SET.
I THINK IT'S TERRIBLE WHEN PEOPLE GIVE THEIR BABY A HYPHENATED LAST NAME LIKE THAT, CATHY.
I DO TOO, MOM.
YOU DO??
IT'S TERRIBLE! THEY ALWAYS PUT THE MAN'S NAME LAST.
WHY CAN'T THEY EVER PUT THE WOMAN'S NAME LAST? WHY CAN'T THE WOMAN BE IN THE "REAL LAST NAME" POSITION, AND THE MAN IN THE PATRONIZED MIDDLE SPOT?!!
WHY DO CHILDREN ONLY AGREE WITH YOU WHEN THEY'RE ON THEIR WAY TO SOMETHING WORSE?
IS THIS A GIFT OR IS IT FOR YOU?
FOR ME? ALL THAT?? OH, NO. HA, HA. NO!
CHOCOLAT
MY BEST FRIEND JUST HAD A BABY. IT'S A GIFT!
WE'RE GOOD FRIENDS OF THE FAMILY. WE'RE BOTH GETTING GIFTS.
YES. GIFTS. GIFTS FOR THE RELATIVES! GIFT-WRAPPED CHOCOLATES FOR THE RELATIVES!!
HOCOLA
HERE'S TO YOU, AUNT CHARLENE.
DITTO, AUNT CATHY.

"MOST NEW-BORNS HAVE A 5-MINUTE ATTENTION SPAN FOR FLASH CARDS."
ANDREA, ZENITH IS ONLY TWO WEEKS OLD!

ZENITH HAS A CURIOUS, RE-CEPTIVE MIND! WHY SHOULD I SIT HERE GOO-ING SENSE-LESSLY WHEN I COULD BE TEACHING HER SOMETHING?!

LOOK, ZENITH! THIS IS SIMONE DE BEAUVOIR... THIS IS THE MONA LISA... THIS IS... IS... OOH, YOU'RE SO CUTE!!

...GOOGLY GOOGLY GA-GA GOOGLY....
..."MOST PAR-ENTS HAVE A 9-SECOND ATTENTION SPAN"....

LUKE'S BUSY CHANGING ZENITH'S DIAPER.
ARE YOU US-ING CLOTH OR DISPOSABLE?

CLOTH DIAPERS ARE MADE OF REUSABLE, NATURAL FIBER. DISPOSABLE DIAPERS ARE SYNTHETIC, NON-BIODEGRAD-ABLE POLLUTANTS!

THERE'S ONLY ONE CHOICE AN ENVIRONMENTALLY AWARE COUPLE CAN MAKE, CATHY.

BUY DISPOSABLE AND SEND A CONTRIBUTION TO GREENPEACE!!
DIAPER PAIL

I WANT US ALL TO LOOK SHARP FOR THE MEETING MONDAY, CATHY. KNOW WHAT I MEAN?
SURE, MR. PINKLEY.
PINKLEY

MEN ARE EXPECTED TO THROW ON A SUIT FROM 1978. WOM-EN ARE EXPECTED TO WEAR A STUNNING NEW OUTFIT.

TO "LOOK SHARP," A MAN HAS TO BRUSH HIS TEETH. A WOM-AN HAS TO SPEND HOURS SHOPPING AND GETTING HER HAIR DONE, NAILS DONE AND MAKEUP DONE!!
PINKLEY

...WHEN MAY I BEGIN?
PINKLEY

IRVING, DO YOU WORSHIP ME, JUST TOLERATE ME, OR "OTHER"?
OTHER.
DO YOU COUNT THE MOMENTS UNTIL YOU SEE ME, NEVER THINK OF ME, OR "OTHER"?
OTHER.
ARE YOU PLANNING OUR FUTURE, OUR BREAK-UP, OR "OTHER"?
OTHER.
HI. I'M CATHY, AND THIS IS MY SIGNIFICANT OTHER.
PARTY COME IN

7:00 AM: TENSE. ANXIOUS. I EAT MY 150-CALORIE LUNCH AND TWO CANDY BARS ON THE WAY TO THE OFFICE.
12:00 NOON: HURRIED AND HASSLED. I DRIVE THROUGH THE "DRIVE-THRU" FOR A CHEESEBURGER AND FRIES.
8:00 P.M.: TIRED AND DEFENSELESS. I HAVE A BURRITO ON THE WAY TO THE CLEANERS... A DOVE BAR ON THE WAY TO AEROBICS... AND HALF A BAG OF GROCERIES ON THE WAY HOME FROM THE STORE.
THE SUMMER OF '86: 90¢ A GALLON AND THREE POUNDS TO THE MILE.
Guisewite

EVERY YEAR I SEE YOU BUY ANOTHER PAIR OF WHITE PANTS AND THEN I NEVER SEE YOU WEAR THEM, CATHY.
PANTS SALE
WHAT HAPPENS? DO YOU GAIN TOO MUCH WEIGHT? GET TOO INSECURE? DO YOU CHANGE YOUR MIND AND RETURN THEM?
WHERE DO THEY ALL GO??
LET'S JUST SAY WE ALL HAVE A FEW SKELETONS IN THE CLOSET, MOM....
...AND MINE ARE ALL WEARING WHITE PANTS.
NEW
Guisewite

YOU REALLY HAVE TO GET THIS REPORT IN, CATHY.
I KNOW. I JUST WANT TO CLEAR A SPACE ON MY DESK FIRST...
IN
...OH. LOOK AT THE DUST. HOLD ON. I'LL JUST WIPE OFF THE DUST...
...AND PUT AWAY THESE FILES ... AND VACUUM UNDER THE CHAIR... AND SORT OUT THIS DRAWER... AND...HOLD ON....
INSIDE EVERY EXECUTIVE THERE'S A CLEANING PERSON SCREAMING TO GET OUT.
Vacuum

HOW ARE WE DOING?
GREAT! I ACTUALLY WROTE PART OF A PRESENTATION WITHOUT THE HELP OF ANY CHOCOLATE!
FITNESS COUNSELOR

I WORE MY SWIMSUIT ONCE WITHOUT CONSOLING MYSELF WITH PIE... AND TWICE IN JULY I'VE DRIVEN PAST FROZEN YOGURT WITHOUT STOPPING!

YOUR RIGHT CALF GREW 3/4."

I DON'T MAKE THE KIND OF PROGRESS YOU CAN MEASURE WITH A TAPE.
TNESS
ELOR
Gruselwitz

"DEAR MIDLAND HIGH SCHOOL GRADUATE... IT'S REUNION TIME!"

"WE'VE FOUND OUR CAREERS, OUR CALLINGS, OUR SPOUSES, OURSELVES, OUR POLITICS, AND OUR RELIGIONS."
HIGH SCHOOL REUNION

" PLEASE JOIN YOUR CLASS IN ACCEPTING ITS BIGGEST CHALLENGE YET: FINDING SUMMER CLOTHES IN JULY."
HIGH SCHOOL REUNION

SUNDRESS! I MUST HAVE A SUNDRESS FOR MY HIGH SCHOOL REUNION!
HOW ABOUT THIS NICE TWEEDY SPORT COAT?
COATS
WOOL
NEW'S FALL ARRIVA
Gruselwitz

WHERE ARE THE SUMMER CLOTHES?! I KNOW YOU HAVE SUMMER CLOTHES BACK THERE!!
BACK WHERE?
COATS
WOOL
BAM BAM
FALL SWEATE

BACK THERE! BACK IN THE SECRET LITTLE ROOM WHERE ALL THE SALESCLERKS HIDE!
FALL

GET AHOLD OF YOURSELF, MISS! SALESCLERKS IN THIS FINE STORE DO NOT HIDE IN A "SECRET LITTLE ROOM" FILLED WITH SUMMER CLOTHES!!

AHEM... SORRY....
THAT'S WHERE THE MANAGER HIDES.
FALL SWEATERS
Gruselwitz

EACH FITNESS PROGRAM IS DESIGNED FOR THE GOALS OF THE INDIVIDUAL.... THIS WOMAN IS PREPARING TO GET INTO WHITE STRETCH PANTS IN AUGUST.
THIGH MACHINE.
COACH

THIS WOMAN IS PREPARING TO MEET HER EX-HUSBAND'S NEW WIFE AT A POOL PARTY.
BUST MACHINE
COACH

THIGH, BUST, REAR, WAIST & ARM MACHINE

OLYMPIC TRIALS?
HIGH SCHOOL REUNION.

OH, HI. DID CATHY RUN TO HER TANNING BOOTH TO GET READY FOR HER HIGH SCHOOL REUNION?
NO. SHE DIDN'T HAVE TIME.

CATHY HAD TO RESORT TO DOING WHAT PEOPLE DID BEFORE THERE WERE TANNING BOOTHS.

YOU DON'T MEAN...
SEE FOR YOURSELF...

YAACK!! I'VE DYED MY LEGS ORANGE!!
JUST LIKE THE GOOD OLD DAYS...

WANT TO BORROW AN OUTFIT OF MINE TO WEAR TO YOUR HIGH SCHOOL REUNION, CATHY?

ANDREA, I'M A SUCCESSFUL BUSINESSWOMAN. DO YOU ACTUALLY THINK I'D TRY TO IMPRESS MY EX-CLASSMATES WITH SOMEONE ELSE'S CLOTHES?!!

SORRY.

MAY I BORROW YOUR HUSBAND AND BABY?

HERE I SIT: GODDESS OF THE TELEPHONE.
click

I COULD INVITE IRVING TO MY HIGH SCHOOL REUNION... OR MAX...OR ALEX... MY WHIM...

...IF I CALL ONE, WILL I WISH I'D CALLED ANOTHER? ...WOULD I RATHER GO ALONE ...I CAN'T DECIDE...I CAN'T COMMIT... I CAN'T MOVE... MY DIALING ARM IS FROZEN....

HERE I SIT: STATUE OF A GODDESS OF THE TELEPHONE.
click

READY FOR THE RAZOR? HA, HA!
THE RAZOR. HA, HA. WHY NOT?

YES. WHY NOT TURN HAIR I LOVE OVER TO A DRUG ADDICT WITH A RAZOR THE WEEK BEFORE MY HIGH SCHOOL REUNION?

GO AHEAD. BUZZ IT! FRIZZ IT! HACK IT! RUIN MY LIFE AND THEN SMILE AND SAY IT WILL "GROW OUT"! HA, HA!

HOW REFRESHING TO FIND SOMEONE SO SURE OF THE NEW STYLE SHE'S GOING TO GET!

snip.

AACK! TOO SHORT! TOO LAYER-Y! AACK! LET ME COUNT THE HAIRS ON THE FLOOR! WHERE'S A MIRROR?!

WHERE'S A LAWYER?! I'LL SUE! NO TIP!! TELL ME IT'S A NIGHTMARE! AACK! I'M FINISHED!!

I'M FINISHED.
FINISHED?! IT DOESN'T LOOK ANY DIFFERENT YET!

GET BACK! NO CLIPPERS! NO COLOR WEAVE! NO SCRUNCHING!!
OH...WAIT. YOU DON'T THINK EVERY-ONE'S HAIR TURNS OUT LIKE MINE, DO YOU?

NO?
HEAVENS NO! I STYLE EACH PERSON'S HAIR TO SUIT HIS OWN FEA-TURES AND LIFESTYLE.

REALLY??
I CUT STOCK-BROKERS' HAIR... DOCTORS' HAIR... I CUT MY OWN MOTHER'S HAIR!

...SO SORRY. PLEASE PROCEED.
HI, MA! JUST PUT LUNCH OVER ON THE COUNTER!
HAIR

HAIR IS TO THE HEAD WHAT FURNITURE IS TO THE HOME, IRVING.
UH, OH.

NO MATTER HOW LONG YOU'VE HAD IT ONE WAY, IT'S NOR-MAL TO WANT TO TOTALLY REARRANGE IT WHEN SEEING PEOPLE YOU HAVEN'T SEEN IN A LONG TIME.

CATHY, WHY DON'T YOU JUST TELL ME YOU GOT A NEW HAIRDO FOR YOUR HIGH SCHOOL REUNION?
IT'S MORE THAN A NEW HAIRDO, IRVING.

I'M HAVING A YARD SALE ON MY HEAD.

MIRACLE WEIGHT LOSS METHODS DO NOT LAST, SWEETIE.
LAST? WHO CARES? I JUST HAVE TO LOOK GOOD FOR THE FOUR HOURS I'M AT MY HIGH SCHOOL RE-UNION, MOM.
FAT DISSOLVER SACK

YOUR NEW SHOES WILL BE OUT OF STYLE IN A MONTH.
SO WHAT? THE SHOES JUST HAVE TO LOOK GOOD FOR FOUR HOURS.
FAT DISSOLVER SACK

I WANT MY DATE, MY FACE, MY BODY AND MY CLOTHES TO LAST FOR FOUR HOURS AND THEN FORGET IT!! BLOOEY!! WHO CARES?!
JUMP JUMP
FAT DISSOLVER SACK
JUMP JUMP

...AND SHE DIDN'T THINK THOSE GOOD HIGH SCHOOL STUDY HABITS WOULD EVER PAY OFF.
FAT DISSOLVER SACK
JUMP
JUMP JUMP

ALL I DID TODAY WAS THINK ABOUT US, IRVING.
WHAT ABOUT ALL YOUR WORK?
I DIDN'T DO ANY WORK. I JUST THOUGHT ABOUT US.
YOU DIDN'T DO ANY WORK?
NO. I DIDN'T DO ANY WORK. DID YOU WORK?
OF COURSE I WORKED. I WAS AT WORK.
YOU COULD WORK??
OF COURSE. I HAD TONS OF WORK.
HOW COULD YOU WORK?
I JUST SAT DOWN AND STARTED WORKING.
MEN HAVE NO ABILITY TO CONCENTRATE.
SILVERSWARTZ

CATHY, YOU'VE DESTROYED YOUR HAIR... DYED YOUR LEGS ORANGE... AND SHAMED YOURSELF IN FIVE STORES PREPARING FOR THIS EVENT...
"PANT PANT"
...AND FOR WHAT? WHY DO YOU EVEN CARE ABOUT SEEING YOUR OLD HIGH SCHOOL GRADUATING CLASS??
HIGH
IT'S JUST SOMETHING I HAVE TO DO, ANDREA.
HIGH SCHOOL REUNION
I WANT TO JOURNEY BACK TO MY HOMETOWN AND STRANGLE THE PERSON WHO ORGANIZED THE REUNION.

WOMAN WAKING UP REMEMBERING A DATE SHE SHOULDN'T HAVE HAD:
NO...
WOMAN WAKING UP REMEMBERING A PIE SHE SHOULDN'T HAVE HAD:
NO...
WOMAN WAKING UP REMEMBERING A PHONE CALL SHE SHOULDN'T HAVE HAD:
NO...
WOMAN WAKING UP REMEMBERING A HAIRCUT SHE SHOULDN'T HAVE HAD:
NO! NO! NO! AACK! NO!!!!

GROW! GROW!! I BEG YOU! PLEASE GROW!
POINK! POINK!
POINK! POINK!
NO! NOT YOU! NOT THE LEGS! NO! SHRINK! SHRINK!!!
BOING BOING BOING BOING BOING
PLOOP
BOING BOING BOING
AAACK!! NOT THE TOP! I DIDN'T WANT THE TOP TO SHRINK!!
SELF-IMAGING: TRIED BY MANY... ...MASTERED BY FEW.

I WISH I COULD JUST HIDE IN THE PARKING LOT WITH A BUNCH OF CLOTHES... WATCH WHAT EVERYONE ELSE WEARS INTO THE REUNION... AND THEN GET DRESSED ACCORDINGLY.
Shoes
Shoes
Shoes
Shoes
Shoes

THAT'S RIDICULOUS. WHAT DOES THE INVITATION SAY ABOUT WHAT TO WEAR?

THE USUAL: "IF CATHY WEARS SOMETHING DRESSY, EVERYONE ELSE IS TO COME IN JEANS. IF CATHY WEARS JEANS, DRESS FORMAL."
MIDLAND HIGH REUNION

READY TO GO, CATHY?
READY.
SHOES
Shoes
Shoes
Shoes
Guisewite

I SHOULD HAVE WORN A DRESS.
MIDLAND HIGH REUNION

NO. MY BLUE SKIRT. MY BLUE SKIRT WOULD HAVE BEEN PERFECT. NO. MY TAN DRESS. DEFINITELY. MY TAN WOULD...

CATHY, WE'RE ALREADY HERE! WOULD YOU QUIT CHANGING YOUR MIND ABOUT WHAT YOU'RE WEARING?!!!

I SHOULD HAVE BROUGHT A DIFFERENT DATE. NO. I SHOULD HAVE COME ALONE. NO. I SHOULD HAVE....
REUNION
Guisewite

IS MY LIPSTICK PERFECT, IRVING?? ELLEN KIMBEL ALWAYS USED TO RIDICULE ME FOR TRYING TO WEAR LIPSTICK IN HIGH SCHOOL.
MIDLAND HIGH REUNION

WHY WOULD YOU WANT TO GO TALK TO A WOMAN WHO USED TO RIDICULE YOU, CATHY??

WHEN SOMEONE'S BEEN THAT PETTY, IT'S IMPORTANT TO FACE HER ONE LAST TIME.
ME

FOR WHAT??
I WANT TO SEE HOW FAT SHE'S GOTTEN.

IMAGINE HOW WE'VE ALL PROGRESSED SINCE WE WERE GIRLS IN HIGH SCHOOL...
MIDLAND HIGH REUNION
WE'VE BECOME SUCCESSFUL, ESTABLISHED, CONFIDENT, WORLDLY, PROUD...
MIDLAND HIGH REUNION
WHO ELSE BUT SOMEONE WHO KNEW US THEN COULD APPRECIATE THE WOMEN WE'VE TURNED INTO ?!
YOU LOOK EXACTLY LIKE YOUR MOTHER.

WHERE WERE YOU IN HIGH SCHOOL?
I WAS THE NERD YOU WOULDN'T TALK TO.

...BUT WHERE WERE YOU IN HIGH SCHOOL?
I WAS THE NERD YOU WOULDN'T TALK TO... ... BUT WHERE WERE YOU?!
I WAS THE NERD YOU WOULDN'T TALK TO.

...BUT WHERE WERE YOU??
PBLLTT!!

THE WONDER OF EVOLUTION: FROM A SCHOOL OF NERDS, A FLOCK OF GEEKS.

IS THIS YOUR HUSBAND, CATHY ?
OH, NO. WE'RE NOT MARRIED.
REUNION

HE'S SINGLE?!
SINGLE MAN?!
THERE'S A SINGLE MAN HERE??!

A SINGLE MAN! IN OUR AGE BRACKET! LEMME SEE! LEMME AT HIM! STAND BACK, I HAVE DIBS!

STILL WORRIED THAT YOU WON'T HAVE ANYONE TO TALK TO, SWEETIE ?

SEE YOU GUYS OUT THERE!
BYE!
LADIES EXIT
MHS REUNIO

WELL. SHE'S HAD A NOSE JOB!
PROBABLY TO GET HER MIND OFF HOW SHE'S BLIMPED OUT!
I THOUGHT SHE WAS P.G.!
IS THAT A WIG, OR WHAT?!
HEE HEE
HEE HEE
HEE
HEE HEE
HEE

...WELL. AHEM....
AHEM.
YES. WELL. AHEM, AHEM...

WHAT'S TAKING SO LONG, CATHY?!
IT'S HARD TO LEAVE FRIENDS LIKE THESE, IRVING.
LADIES
TAP TAP

SARAH CAN NAME ALL THE PEOPLE WHO WERE IN THE YEATS PAGEANT IN MRS. TOOLER'S ENGLISH CLASS IN THE TENTH GRADE.
YOU'RE KIDDING.

I DON'T EVEN REMEMBER THE YEATS PAGEANT.
I DON'T REMEMBER YEATS OR MRS. TOOLER.

I DON'T REMEMBER YEATS, TOOLER, SARAH OR TAKING ENGLISH!
AND WHO EXACTLY ARE YOU??!

COMPETITIVE SENILITY... IT WAS JUST A MATTER OF TIME...

ARE YOU MARRIED YET, CATHY?
NO.
class of 2005

NO??
NO. I'M SURE YOU AND YOUR HUSBAND ARE VERY HAPPY... ..BUT I HAVE THE ROMANCE OF THE UNKNOWN...
class of 2005

...THE EXHILARATION OF FEELING THAT EVERY NEW ENCOUNTER MAY BE THE BEGINNING OF A GRAND AND GLORIOUS PASSION!!
class of 2005

ARE YOU MARRIED YET, CATHY?
YES.
class of 2005

ALL WE EVER CARED ABOUT IN HIGH SCHOOL WAS, "WILL I GET A DATE?"
YEAH...OR, "CAN I BORROW THE CAR?"
MIDLAND HIGH REUNION

OR, "WHERE'S MY ALLOWANCE?"
ALL "ME, ME, ME."
MIDLAND HIGH REUNION

HOW REWARDING TO FINALLY BE AT THE STAGE WHERE OUR CARES GO BEYOND OUR OWN LIVES TO THE FAR MORE UNIVERSAL QUESTIONS...

HOW DID BOBBY EWING GET IN THAT SHOWER ??!
MIDLAND HIGH REUNION

SHE SAID, "YOU CAN'T GO OUT IN A SKIRT THAT TIGHT!"...LIKE I'M STILL A KID!!
YEAH, HA, HA! MINE DOES THAT, TOO!
MIDLAND HIGH REUNION

I THINK MINE WOULD ACTUALLY CALL THE POLICE IF I WEREN'T HOME BY MIDNIGHT!
I KNOW. HA, HA! THEY'RE ALL THE SAME!

YEAH....HA, HA!... ..HERE. I HAVE A PICTURE OF LITTLE JENNIFER RIGHT HERE!
OH, DEAR.

THEY'RE TALKING ABOUT THEIR DAUGHTERS. I WAS TALKING ABOUT MY MOTHER.

I JUST SAW RICKY, CATHY.
RICKY?? RICKY'S HERE??

ALL YOU COULD SAY WHEN YOU HEARD HIS NAME IN HIGH SCHOOL WAS, "HOW DOES MY HAIR LOOK?? HOW DOES MY HAIR LOOK??"

ISN'T IT GREAT THAT YOU CAN FACE HIM TODAY WITH MORE ON YOUR MIND THAN "HOW DOES MY HAIR LOOK?"!
YEAH...

HOW DO MY WRINKLES LOOK?

IT'S BEEN A GOOD SUMMER, BUT SORT OF A CONFUSING ONE, IRVING. WE SEE EACH OTHER...WE DON'T SEE EACH OTHER...
THEN I THINK WE'RE BREAKING UP...THEN I THINK, NO. THIS IS IT. WE'RE REALLY BECOMING A UNIT. THEN I THINK I LIKE THAT. THEN I THINK, NO. TOO SOON. TOO PARANOID. THEN, NO. I LIKE THIS. IT'S NICE. IT'S RIGHT. THEN, NO. THEN, YES. THEN I DON'T KNOW, YOU KNOW?
YEAH. ME TOO.
I KEEP SENDING LETTERS AND GETTING BACK POSTCARDS.

CATHY ?? THAT'S YOU ?? CATHY ??!
HELLO.
MHS REUNION

I CAN'T BELIEVE IT! YOU'RE... BEAUTIFUL!
YES. YOU BLEW IT, RICKY.

I DIDN'T KNOW YOU'D TURN OUT LIKE....WAIT... I MEAN...WAIT! ...CAN WE HAVE LUNCH...CATHY!..
REGARDS TO THE WIFE. HI TO THE KIDS.

WE CAN GO HOME NOW, IRVING. I'VE MADE SOMEONE SICK.

I REALLY LOVED HAVING YOU AT MY HIGH SCHOOL REUNION, IRVING, BUT NOW I NEED A LITTLE TIME ALONE.
I UNDERSTAND.

I FACED SO MANY OLD FRIENDS AND EMOTIONS TO-NIGHT.... IT'S TIMES LIKE THIS THAT A WOMAN REALLY NEEDS TO JUST BE WITH HERSELF FOR A WHILE.

IT'S OK, CATHY. DO WHAT YOU HAVE TO DO.
THANK YOU, IRVING.

EAT
Chomp chomp EAT EAT
GOBBBLE
chomp EAT EAT EAT
NUTS
chocolate
cookies

I COULD SLOWLY PRY FOR DETAILS ON CATHY'S CLASS REUNION, CAUSING MANY SMALL CONFRONTATIONS...

OR I COULD GET IT ALL OVER WITH IN ONE SURPRISE BLITZ.
knock

HOW WAS THE REUNION? ANY HOT PROSPECTS? ANY LEADS? ANY LOOKERS? ANY LIVE ONES? STILL SPEAKING TO IRVING? ANYONE NEW?
AACK! AACK! NO! NO! YES! YES! NO! AACK!

THE "RIPPING OFF THE BAND-AID" SCHOOL OF MOTHERHOOD.

MY HIGH SCHOOL REUNION BROUGHT BACK SO MANY MEMORIES... RIDING MY BIKE TO McCANDLESS BOOKSTORE TO LOOK AT ALL THE NEW CARDS AND BOOKS AND GIFTS...

...STOPPING AT SWANSON'S FOR CANDY... GOING TO NUGENTS FOR A SODA...WANDERING AROUND HANSEN'S DEPARTMENT STORE...CURTIS BAKERY...LEMPKE'S BOOTERY...CITY DAIRY ICE CREAM...

THESE ARE MY RICHEST MEMORIES, ANDREA... MY FOUNDATION... IT'S WHO I AM... WHERE I CAME FROM... IT'S EVERYTHING I CARE ABOUT... IT'S..IT'S...

IT'S FOOD AND SHOPPING.
...FOOD AND SHOPPING....

CATHY, WILL YOU...
THAT DOES IT. I CAN'T WORK WITH ALL THESE INTERRUPTIONS.

FROM NOW ON, NO ONE IS TO WALK THROUGH THIS DOOR! NO ONE IS TO KNOCK ON, OPEN OR WALK THROUGH THIS DOOR! NO EXCEPTIONS! THIS DOOR STAYS CLOSED!!!

SLAM

I HAVE TO GO TO THE BATHROOM.

I THOUGHT YOUR WEIRD HAIRDO WOULD GO AWAY AFTER YOUR HIGH SCHOOL REUNION, CATHY.
NO SUCH LUCK, CHARLENE.

MY SLIM NEW SHAPE DISAPPEARED...MY BEAUTIFUL NAILS ARE GONE FOREVER... ..ALL IMPROVEMENTS INSTANTLY VANISHED.

ONLY THE WEIRD, HORRIBLE HAIRDO IS STILL WITH ME.

THE ONES YOU HOPE YOU NEVER HEAR FROM AGAIN ARE THE ONES WHO NEVER LOSE YOUR ADDRESS.

I'LL HAVE SOME MORE OF THOSE CRACKERS, CATHY.
THE CRACKERS ARE GONE, IRVING.
YOU ATE A PLATE OF CRACKERS BETWEEN THE PORCH AND THE LIVING ROOM??
YES. AND I ATE ALL THE CHEESE ON THE WAY TO THE KITCHEN.
AND IN THE TWO STEPS BETWEEN THE COUNTER AND THE GARBAGE DISPOSAL, I POLISHED OFF THE GUACAMOLE.
I CAN'T BELIEVE THIS.
ME EITHER. I HAVE TO FIND A SMALLER APARTMENT.
I DON'T KNOW WHY YOU'RE COMPLAINING, CATHY. WOMEN DON'T HAVE TO SHAVE EVERY DAY.
NO, WE DON'T.
BEACH
INSTEAD, WE CAN POUR HOT WAX OVER OUR LEGS, LET IT DRY AND THEN RIP THE HAIR OUT WITH THE HARDENED WAX... WE CAN SMEAR OUR LEGS WITH CHEMICALS STRONG ENOUGH TO ACTUALLY DISSOLVE THE HAIR....
...OR, WE CAN PAY SOME STRANGER TO ELECTROCUTE EACH OF THE 7 BILLION HAIRS ONE BY ONE BY ONE..
OK, OK!! ENOUGH! BLEAH
IT'S SORT OF LIKE LIFE, IRVING... IT ONLY SEEMS AS IF WOMEN HAVE MORE OPTIONS.
MY HUSBAND SAID THE CUTEST THING....
WE SWORE WE'D NEVER DO THAT TO EACH OTHER, ANDREA. REMEMBER?
I KNOW YOUR HUSBAND'S NAME... YOU KNOW YOUR HUSBAND'S NAME... THERE'S NO REASON TO RUB IN THE FACT THAT YOU HAVE A HUSBAND AND I DONT BY REFERRING TO HIM AS "MY HUSBAND"!!
SORRY, CATHY.
THANK YOU.
THE FATHER OF MY BABY SAID THE CUTEST THING....

HOW DO YOU KEEP YOUR HOUSE SO NEAT WITH A NEW BABY HERE, ANDREA?
IT'S SIMPLE ORGANIZATION, CATHY.

THIS IS OUR WORK SPACE... THIS IS OUR FOOD PREPARATION SPACE... THIS IS OUR LEARNING SPACE...
creak

FWOMP!!

THIS IS OUR "STUFF-EVERYTHING-IN-HERE-WHEN-COMPANY-COMES-OVER" SPACE.

ZENITH'S CRYING. I KNEW SHE'D BE INSULTED BY THE ENGLISH TRANSLATION OF "IL TROVATORE."
I THINK SHE'S MAD THAT WE MOVED THE BRAQUE PRINT FROM HER ROOM.
WAAH!!

NO. SHE'S SCREAMING BECAUSE WE WOULDN'T LET HER CHEW ON THE AFRICAN SOAPSTONE.
SHE'S BORED. SHE WANTS A FRENCH LESSON.
SHE WANTS HER HAND-LOOMED AUSTRALIAN TREE HAMMOCK...NO, HER...
WAAH!

burp.
PAT

SHE WAS REQUESTING THE ANCIENT INTERNATIONAL POST-FEEDING RITUAL.
Guisewitz

I LOVE THE HAT, CATHY.
YOU DO?

OH, YES. THE ABILITY TO WEAR A HAT SAYS SO MUCH ABOUT A WOMAN.
LUNC

"I'M CONFIDENT!" "I'M PROUD!"

"I'VE JUST TAKEN A HIDEOUS HAIRCUT AND MADE IT WORSE BY GETTING A PERM."
Guisewitz

HOW BAD IS IT, ANDREA?
IT'S BAD, CATHY.

MY MOTHER SAYS IT'S CUTE.
YOUR MOTHER WOULD SAY A GARBAGE CAN ON YOUR HEAD WAS CUTE.

NO MATTER HOW RIDICULOUS THE REST OF THE WORLD THINKS YOU LOOK, YOUR MOTHER SAYS YOU'RE CUTE SO YOU'LL LOVE HER.. IT'S JUST A TRICK YOUR MOTHER USES TO MAKE SURE YOU LOVE HER!

IT'S WORKING.

I HAVE A $200 SKIN CARE SYSTEM ON THE COUNTER AND I'M STANDING IN THE SHOWER WASHING MY FACE WITH DEODORANT SOAP.

I'M SIX INCHES FROM A REFRIGERATOR OF FRESH VEGETABLES. HERE I SIT, EATING CHOCOLATE CHIP MUFFINS.
INS

SURROUNDED BY NEWSPAPERS, FINE NOVELS AND CLASSICAL MUSIC, I PROP MY FEET ON THE COLLECTED WORKS OF SHAKESPEARE AND WATCH "THE LOVE CONNECTION".

PERFECTION IS WITHIN MY REACH, BUT JUST SLIGHTLY OUT OF MY GRASP.

YOUR HAIR IS ALL FLATTENED DOWN AND BACK TO NORMAL, CATHY. HOW IS THAT POSSIBLE?!
LET'S JUST SAY THAT IN A WORLD WHERE BOBBY EWING CAN COME BACK TO LIFE, ANYTHING'S POSSIBLE.

LET'S JUST SAY THAT IF FALLON COULD SHOW UP IN DENVER WITH A NEW FACE, I CAN BE HERE WITH NEW HAIR.

LET'S JUST SAY THAT IN 1986, IN THE WIDE SCREEN OF LIFE, WE ALL MAKE OUR OWN LITTLE REALITIES, CHARLENE...

LET'S JUST SAY THAT SOMEONE CASHED IN HER IRA ON A BATHROOM FULL OF HAIR SPRAY.
THANK YOU, MOTHER.

I'VE BEEN WAITING FOR TONIGHT FOR SO LONG, CATHY...
ME TOO, IRVING... LET'S MOVE TO THE COUCH...
OH, YEAH... THIS IS MORE LIKE IT...
WHAT?! AACK. WHAT ARE YOU DOING ?? DON'T DO THAT !
I'VE WAITED FOR MONTHS TO FIND OUT IF SAM PROPOSED TO DIANE ON "CHEERS," AND I'M NOT GOING TO HAVE MY SPECIAL MOMENT RUINED BECAUSE YOU'RE KISSING ME !!!
INCREDIBLE.
HOLD MY HAND, HONEY. THIS WILL BE SO ROMANTIC.

THIS WORD IS "WOMAN," ZENITH. WHEN MOMMY WAS LITTLE, ALL WOMEN DID WAS TAKE CARE OF BABIES.
CAT
TOY
WOMAN

OH, BUT WHAT A WORLD I HAVE TO SHOW YOU NOW!! CAREERS! OPPORTUNITIES! CHALLENGES! ACHIEVEMENTS! OH, ZENITH, I CAN'T WAIT TO BE YOUR ROLE MODEL!!!
CAT

WHEN ARE YOU GOING TO GO BACK TO WORK, ANDREA?
WHAT, AND LEAVE MY BABY??!!

THIS WORD IS "CONTRADICTION." ONE OF THE BIGGIES...
CAT
TOY
CONTRADICTION

WE'LL PAY YOU TO BABY-SIT FOR ZENITH ON FRIDAY.
PAY? DON'T BE SILLY. I'M HAPPY TO DO IT.

THIS WILL BE THE FIRST TIME I'VE BEEN AWAY FROM HER SINCE THE MOMENT OF CONCEPTION, CATHY.

ZENITH IS OUR LIFE. SHE'S EVERYTHING WE CARE ABOUT. YOU'RE THE ONLY PERSON IN THE WORLD TO WHOM WE WOULD TRUST OUR FRAGILE, TINY TREASURE. OUR BABY. OUR JOY. OUR WORLD. THE REASON FOR LIFE ITSELF.

PLEASE LET US PAY YOU SOMETHING.
$75,000.00 A MINUTE.

JUST FLING THE JUNK OFF THE COUCH AND HAVE A SEAT, IRVING. I'M JUST STUFFING THE LAUNDRY IN THE BROOM CLOSET...

...THROWING OUT THE DEAD PLANTS... I'LL STICK SOME CARRY-OUT CHICKEN IN THE MICROWAVE...GRAB A CARROT...BING! THERE. DINNER!

WHAT DID YOU WANT TO TALK ABOUT?
OH, I WONDERED IF YOU'D LIKE TO BABY-SIT ANDREA AND LUKE'S BABY WITH ME TOMORROW NIGHT.
chicken

WHY WOULD YOU WANT ME THERE?
I WANT YOU TO GET TO SEE HOW MATERNAL I AM.
chicken

LUKE AND I WILL BE LEAVING ZENITH WITH YOU FOR EXACTLY TWO HOURS. WE'LL HAVE A CELLULAR PHONE WITH US AT ALL TIMES, AND WE'RE BOTH WEARING BEEPERS.

I PROGRAMMED THE COMPUTER TO ELECTRONICALLY TRACK OUR CAR, WITH ONE-DIGIT DIALING FOR EVERY HOME BETWEEN HERE AND THE RESTAURANT.

WE'LL CHECK IN EVERY HALF-HOUR. IF YOU DON'T ANSWER BY THE THIRD RING, WE PUSH THIS BUTTON, WHICH INSTANTANEOUSLY SENDS THE PARAMEDICS, IN-LAWS, AND, OF COURSE, OUR OWN SWAT TEAM.
TWEET!

ARE YOU SURE YOU WANT TO GO OUT?
OH, YES! WE NEED AN EVENING TO JUST RELAX.
WATER

SHE'S GOING TO START WAILING THE SECOND WE LEAVE, CATHY.
NO, SHE WON'T. MOMMY TOLD HER ALL ABOUT TONIGHT.

SHE'S GOING TO START WAILING THE SECOND WE LEAVE.
NO, SHE WON'T. MOMMY'S BIG GIRL WON'T WAIL, WILL SHE? NO!

WAAA!!

SHE STARTED WAILING THE SECOND WE LEFT.
WAAA!! COME TO MAMA!!

WAVE BYE BYE, ZENITH!
AACK! I CAN'T LEAVE MY BABY!

SEE THE FUNNY FACE MOMMY'S MAKING? BYE BYE, FUNNY MOMMY!
LET ME GO, LUKE! I CAN'T LEAVE MY BABY!!

AACK! MY BABY! I'M HERE, BABY!!

WAAAH!!
WE CAN'T LEAVE NOW, LUKE. SHE'S TOO UPSET.

YOU COULDN'T LEAVE ZENITH FOR **TWO HOURS** TONIGHT, ANDREA?? WHAT'S HAPPENED TO YOU?!
OVER-BOND-ING.
OVERBONDING?
THE PARENT GETS SO ATTACHED TO THE BABY THAT SHE TOTALLY DISTORTS WHAT MIGHT HAPPEN IF SHE ISN'T WITH HER 24 HOURS A DAY.
IT'S IRRATIONAL, HYSTERICAL BEHAVIOR THAT I CAN'T **BELIEVE** I GAVE IN TO. ZENITH IS AS STRONG AND HEALTHY AS A TWO-MONTH-OLD CAN BE!
WHY DON'T YOU JUST GO CHANGE CLOTHES?
WHAT IF SHE STARTS WALKING WHILE I'M IN THE BEDROOM??!!

I'M BACK! I FINALLY DECIDED IT'S TIME FOR THIS NEW MOMMY TO EASE BACK INTO THE WORK FORCE!
HOW NICE FOR YOU.
PERSONNEL

I THINK I'D LIKE TO START A FEW HOURS A DAY... BUILD TO A 30-HOUR WEEK... OF COURSE GOING HOME TO NURSE OR BRINGING ZENITH HERE FOR LUNCH!
ISN'T THAT SWEET.

THEN MAYBE THE CHAIRMAN OF THE BOARD WILL COME SKIPPING DOWN THE HALL WITH BASKETS OF TOYS FOR ALL THE CHILDREN WHILE OUR CLIENTS SING LULLABYE DUETS IN THE RECEPTION AREA!!

SORRY. I WAS BEING A LITTLE UNREALISTIC. I'D LIKE TO COME BACK TO WORK.
WE GAVE AWAY YOUR JOB LAST MONTH.
PERSONNEL

THERE USED TO BE NO MATERNITY LEAVE, NO PATERNITY LEAVE, NO FLEXTIME AND NO COMPANY DAY CARE.
PERSONNEL

BUT WE PLEDGED TO CHANGE ALL THAT! TO PAVE THE WAY FOR THE NEXT GENERATION OF WOMEN!

WELL, HERE SHE IS! ZENITH! THE NEXT GENERATION OF WOMEN!

WE HAVE NO MATERNITY LEAVE, NO PATERNITY LEAVE, NO FLEXTIME AND NO DAY CARE.
WE'RE NOT QUITE READY FOR YOU YET.
PERSONNEL

HOW COULD YOU GIVE MY JOB AWAY?!
COMPANIES AREN'T REQUIRED TO HOLD JOBS FOR WOMEN WHO TAKE TIME OFF TO HAVE BABIES, ANDREA.
PERSONNEL

THAT'S RIDICULOUS! 44% OF THE WHOLE LABOR FORCE IS WOMEN, AND 80% OF US WILL HAVE CHILDREN! THIS IS 1986!!

LET'S JUST SAY THIS COMPANY BELIEVES IN OLD-FASHIONED VALUES.

WHAT??
THEY FOUND SOMEONE WHO WOULD TAKE YOUR JOB FOR A 1950 SALARY.
PERSONNEL

EVERY INDUSTRIALIZED NATION IN THE WORLD PROVIDES MATERNITY LEAVE UP TO A YEAR EXCEPT AMERICA, WHERE A WOMAN CAN LOSE HER JOB FOR TAKING MORE THAN TWO WEEKS OFF TO GIVE BIRTH ??!!
ADMINISTRATION
AN UGLY EXAGGERATION. OFTEN WE GIVE HER THE JOB BACK, BUT JUST TAKE AWAY ALL SENIORITY... SOMETIMES WE GIVE BACK HER TITLE, BUT REMOVE ALL STATUS, AUTHORITY AND HOPE FOR ADVANCEMENT.
ADMINISTRATION
OF COURSE, WE'D MUCH RATHER NOT LET A NEW MOTHER GO.
WELL, THAT'S GOOD TO HEAR.
ADMINISTRATION
IF SHE QUITS ON HER OWN, WE CAN SKIP THE WHOLE SEVERANCE PAY FIASCO!
ADMINISTRATION
MOST WOMEN NEED THE INCOME OF A FULL-TIME JOB, BUT DAY CARE COSTS ALMOST AS MUCH AS THEY CAN EARN.
PERSONNEL
IF COMPANIES DON'T HELP WITH MATERNITY LEAVE OR CHILD CARE, IT'S HOPELESS.
IT'S LIKE SAYING ONLY RICH PEOPLE CAN HAVE CHILDREN!!
NO ONE'S SAYING ONLY RICH PEOPLE CAN HAVE CHILDREN.
THANK YOU.
ONLY RICH PEOPLE CAN HAVE JOBS.
PERSONNEL
IF THE "FAMILY AND MEDICAL LEAVE ACT" COULD REALLY GUARANTEE MATERNITY LEAVES, WHY AREN'T THERE BIG DEMONSTRATIONS FOR IT?
BY WHOM, CATHY?
THE PEOPLE MOST DESPERATE FOR THE BILL ARE SIMULTANEOUSLY RECOVERING FROM BIRTH, WORKING FULL TIME, CARING FOR A NEWBORN, AND DOING ALL THE SHOPPING, COOKING AND CLEANING FOR A HUSBAND AND ONE OR MORE OTHER CHILDREN! WHO'S GOING TO DEMONSTRATE?
WHY DON'T THEY WRITE LETTERS?
FAMILY AND MEDICAL LEAVE
COULD YOU WRITE YOUR CONGRESSPERSON TONIGHT?
YEAH...RIGHT AFTER I WHIP OFF A NOTE TO THE QUEEN OF ENGLAND.

A PIECE OF CHEESE.
A PAN OF CINNAMON ROLLS AND A BOWL OF FROSTING.
AN APPLE.
A TUB OF MACARONI SALAD.
MINERAL WATER.
A CHOCOLATE SODA.
ICE CUBES.
FROZEN ÉCLAIRS AND A CAKE.
HOW CAN TWO PEOPLE GET SUCH DIFFERENT THINGS OUT OF THE SAME RELATIONSHIP?
CHOCOLA ICE CREAM
Éclairs
Chocolate Soda
CAKE
Chocolate Syrup
Groening

WHILE I WAS HERE, HAPPILY TEACHING FRENCH VERB CONJUGATIONS TO MY TWO-MONTH-OLD, THEY GAVE MY JOB AWAY!
JE PEUX
TU PEUX
ELLE PEUT
NOUS POUVONS
THEY GAVE YOUR JOB AWAY?
I STILL CAN'T BELIEVE IT! I SHOULD HAVE KNOWN BETTER.
JE PEUX
ELLE PEUT
NOUS POUVONS
YOU'RE USUALLY NOT SO SHORT-SIGHTED, ANDREA.
I KNOW.
I SHOULD HAVE TAUGHT HER SWEDISH. IN SWEDEN EVERYONE GETS A ONE-YEAR MATERNITY LEAVE WITH PAY.
GUISEWITE

ATTENTION ALL EMPLOYEES: THE BETS HAVE BEEN TALLIED ON LAST WEEK'S "GUESS THE CLIFFHANGER OUTCOME" CONTEST!
ALL "DYNASTY," "DALLAS," "COLBYS" AND "KNOTS LANDING" LOSERS, PLEASE BRING CASH OR MONEY ORDERS PAYABLE TO CHARLENE.....
THAT DOES IT, CHARLENE.
CHARLENE
THIS IS AN OFFICE! WOULD YOU QUIT WASTING TIME ON THAT DRIVEL AND TAKE CARE OF SOME BUSINESS?!
ATTENTION ALL EMPLOYEES: THE BETS HAVE BEEN TALLIED ON YESTERDAY'S RAMS-EAGLES GAME. PLEASE BRING CASH OR MONEY ORDERS PAYABLE TO MR. PINKLEY.....
MUCH BETTER.
GUISEWITE

DID I WASH THIS ONE BEFORE I STUFFED IT IN THE DRAWER LAST YEAR? NO. DID I WASH THIS ONE? NO. THIS ONE? NO. THIS ONE? NO. THIS ONE? NO.
FILTHY SWEATERS: THE APARTMENT DWELLER'S LEAF PILE.
GUISEWITE

THIS YEAR I'M REALLY GOING TO LOOK BEFORE I BUY FALL CLOTHES, CATHY!
ME TOO, MOM!
I WILL BUY NO FADS!
NO UNMATCHED SEPARATES!
NOTHING I HAVE TO HAND WASH!!
NOTHING I HAVE TO LOSE WEIGHT TO WEAR!!
...AAACK! THIS IS ADORABLE! I MUST HAVE THIS! I'LL LOSE WEIGHT! I'LL WASH IT! I'LL MATCH IT! I'LL TAKE IT!!
WHY DO YOU EVEN BOTHER WITH THE BIG PEP TALK?
IT'S SORT OF LIKE SINGING THE NATIONAL ANTHEM BEFORE A FOOTBALL GAME.
GUISEWITE

I KNOW EXACTLY HOW THIS COMPANY SHOULD BE RUN. NO ONE ASKS.
IN
I KNOW PRECISELY WHAT THEY CAN DO WITH BANKS, INSURANCE COMPANIES, POLLUTION, THE ARMS RACE AND THE "NEW FALL SILHOUETTE." NO ONE ASKS.
IN
I DON'T HAVE THE SLIGHTEST IDEA WHAT MY FUTURE WILL BE WITH IRVING, OR THE VAGUEST CLUE ABOUT HOW WE MIGHT MAKE IT WORK. EVERYONE ASKS.
IN
PEOPLE ONLY LOOK IN THE CUPBOARDS THAT ARE A MESS.
GUISEWITE

IT'S FUNNY HOW WE WORRY ABOUT DIFFERENT PARTS OF OUR BODIES AT DIFFERENT TIMES OF OUR LIVES.
A BIGGER BUST! FLATTER REAR! ROUNDER REAR! SLIMMER LEGS! TEENSY WAIST!
NOW I LOOK AT MYSELF, AND IT ALL SEEMS KIND OF SILLY, MOM.
I KNOW, SWEETIE.
NOW I WANT SILICONE INJECTIONS IN THE SHOULDERS.
GUISEWITE

DO YOU EVER TALK TO MAX ANYMORE, CATHY?
NO. I GOT SO TIRED OF COMPETING WITH HIS COMPUTER FOR ATTENTION.
RECEPTIONIST

HE'S NOT MY TYPE. NOT MY KIND. NICE, BUT NO MAGIC. NO CHEMISTRY. JUST NOT THERE. NOT HAPPENING. NO WAY. NOT FOR ME. NO. HUH, UH. NO. NO, DEFINITELY NO.

HE'S GETTING MARRIED.
RECEPTIONIST

...EEEEAAACKKK!
WHAT WAS THAT?!
THE SOUND OF A BRAIN SWITCHING TRACKS AT 200 M.P.H.
RECEPTIONIST
GUISEWITE

MORE DIET COLA.
AND KEEP IT COMING.

LET ME GUESS. ANOTHER GIRLFRIEND IS GETTING MARRIED.
OH, PLEASE.

THERE ARE THINGS IN LIFE A LOT MORE IMPORTANT THAN GIRLFRIENDS GETTING MARRIED!

SORRY.
OUR BOYFRIENDS ARE STARTING TO GET MARRIED!!
GUISEWITE

SO WHAT IF MAX IS GETTING MARRIED, CATHY? HE WASN'T RIGHT FOR YOU.
I KNOW.

DEEP DOWN, I STILL FEEL THERE'S ONE SPECIAL MAN OUT THERE FOR ALL OF US.

YEAH, ME TOO..

...ONE MAN FOR ALL OF US.
GUISEWITE

MAX IS GETTING MARRIED, MOM. LET'S SEE...THAT MAKES:
RICHARD: MARRIED
MARK: MARRIED
PAUL: ENGAGED
GRANT: ON THE BRINK...

YOU KEEP A MENTAL RECORD OF THE MARITAL STATUS OF EVERYONE YOU'VE EVER DATED, CATHY??
WHAT'S WRONG WITH THAT?

I'M SURPRISED YOU EVEN REMEMBER! YOU HAVEN'T SEEN SOME OF THOSE PEOPLE IN YEARS!
I GUESS IT IS SORT OF SILLY.

CROSS MAX OFF THE MASTER CHART, DEAR!
CRAIG
BRIAN
ROBERT
LES
RICHARD
CHRIS
TONY
PAUL
JEFF
ALEX
MAX
JOEY
MARK
EMER
DRA
TODD
IRV
HOT LINE
GUISEWITE

CATHY, IF YOU LIKED MAX SO MUCH, WHY DIDN'T YOU PURSUE HIM WHEN YOU HAD THE CHANCE?
I THOUGHT THERE WAS PLENTY OF TIME, MOM.

YOU PROCRASTINATED ?? ON SOMETHING LIKE THAT ?!!
OH, LOOK WHO'S TALKING.

YOU PUT EVERYTHING OFF UNTIL LATER! MENDING... BILLS...SHOPPING...READING... NOTES...LOOK AROUND, MOM!
I SEE.
GUISEWITE

OUR DAUGHTER WILL NEVER MARRY OR BEAR CHILDREN BECAUSE I LET THE MAIL STACK UP ON THE COUNTER.

ALL WEEK IT SEEMED AS IF I WAS RUNNING IN THE WRONG DIRECTION.

EVERYONE WAS HERE... I WAS OVER THERE....

NOW IT'S THE WEEKEND, AND I CAN FINALLY COLLECT MYSELF ALL IN ONE PLACE.

AT LAST...I'M IN SINK WITH THE REST OF THE WORLD.

IT'S TOO BAD ABOUT YOUR FRIEND MAX GETTING MARRIED, CATHY.
MOM, YOU DIDN'T EVEN LIKE MAX.

I LOVED MAX! I JUST ACTED COOL BECAUSE I THOUGHT YOU DIDN'T CARE FOR HIM.
I ACTED AS IF I WANTED YOU TO BECAUSE YOU WANTED ME TO!!

WHAT?! I ONLY DISAPPROVED BECAUSE I THOUGHT YOU WANTED ME TO!
I ACTED AS IF I WANTED YOU TO BECAUSE YOU WANTED ME TO!!

WHAT??
EVEN WHEN WE TALK RIGHT AT EACH OTHER, WE GET THE INFORMATION FOURTH HAND.

IT'S A BEAUTIFUL, SUNNY DAY OUT. THIS IS WAY TOO HEAVY TO WEAR.

THIS IS TOO LIGHT.

TOO HEAVY...TOO LIGHT...TOO HEAVY...TOO LIGHT...TOO HEAVY...TOO LIGHT.....

THE ONE DAY THAT I'M THE RIGHT SIZE, MY CLOTHES ALL HAVE A WEIGHT PROBLEM.

THE "BIG LOOK" MAKES ME LOOK LIKE AN ELEPHANT. DON'T YOU HAVE ANYTHING ELSE?
CERTAINLY.
NEW
FALL

THIS YEAR YOU CAN WEAR THE "BIG LOOK" THAT MAKES YOU LOOK LIKE AN ELEPHANT... OR YOU CAN WEAR THE "SKIN-TIGHT LOOK" AND LOOK LIKE AN ELEPHANT ON YOUR OWN!
FALL

WOULD YOU RATHER HAVE YOUR FAT IMPLIED BY THE OUTFIT--THE "PASSIVE FAT" APPROACH....OR WOULD YOU RATHER SHOW THAT FAT FOR WHAT IT IS IN A CLINGY KNIT--THE "ASSERTIVE FAT" APPROACH?!

WHATEVER HAPPENED TO THE GOOD OLD DAYS WHEN THE CHOICES WERE BLUE AND GREEN?

I SHOULD TRY GOING OUT WITH OTHER PEOPLE BESIDES IRVING, BUT I'M TOO FAT TO MEET SOMEONE NEW.
Life
Sports
I'D HATE TO WASTE A WHOLE TRIAL SEPARATION TRYING TO LOSE WEIGHT.
Life
BETTER TO STAY WITH IRVING UNTIL I LOSE 15 POUNDS AND THEN START GOING OUT.
Life
WHOEVER WOULD HAVE THOUGHT THAT MY FAT WOULD BE KEEPING US TOGETHER ?...
Life

AREN'T THESE GREAT, MOM?
YOUR FATHER AND I PAID AS MUCH FOR OUR FIRST CAR AS THOSE BOOTS COST, CATHY.

THESE ARE CUTE...
MY WEDDING DRESS COST LESS THAN THAT PAIR OF GYM SHOES.

THESE...?
THOSE PUMPS COST AS MUCH AS THE WASHER I USED FOR THE FIRST SIX YEARS OF OUR MARRIAGE.

ANY LUCK?
SHE WOULDN'T TRY ANY ON.
Shoes

CATHY, THIS SWEATER COSTS $125!!
BETTER TO HAVE ONE GREAT SWEATER THAN A BUNCH OF CHEAP ONES I DON'T LIKE, MOM.

REMEMBER THE $30 DRESS I BOUGHT ONCE AND NEVER WORE?

YOU BRING UP THAT SAME $30 MISTAKE EVERY YEAR AND THEN RATIONALIZE SPENDING EVEN MORE MONEY ON CLOTHES YOU DON'T WEAR!

OUTFITS COME AND GO, BUT A GOOD BLUNDER GETS USED FOREVER.
SALES DESK

HERE. YOU NEED TO ADD SHOULDER PADS TO BALANCE THE HIPS...

...A WIDE BELT TO BALANCE THE SHOULDERS... BUNCHY LEGGINGS TO BALANCE THE BELT... FRINGY BOOTS TO BALANCE THE LEGGINGS....

...THERE! SEE WHAT A LITTLE IMAGINATION CAN DO??

I'VE GAINED 25 POUNDS WITHOUT EATING ANYTHING.

HI! HOW WAS YOUR WEEKEND?
YAK
YAK, YAK YAK,
RECEPTIONIST

HI! HOW WAS YOUR WEEKEND?
YAK YAK, YAK, YAK YAK, YAK,
RECEPTIONIST

CHARLENE, YOU'VE SPENT THE WHOLE MORNING ASKING PEOPLE HOW THEIR WEEKEND WAS! ISN'T IT TIME TO START DOING SOMETHING ELSE?!!

HI! HOW WAS YOUR LUNCH?
YAK
YAK, YAK YAK,

AAAAAAAACK
CATHY

CATHY

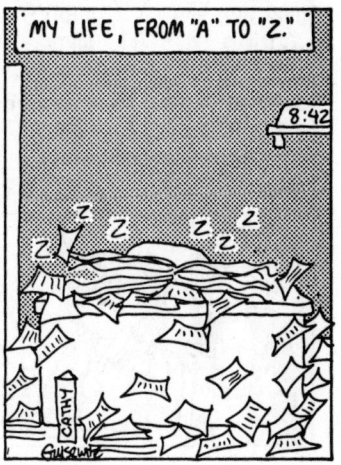
MY LIFE, FROM "A" TO "Z."
8:42
CATHY

WHEN I SPENT $300 ON THIS SUIT LAST YEAR, YOU TOLD ME I COULD JUST UPDATE IT EVERY YEAR WITH A NEW ACCESSORY.
Boutique

BUT EVERYTHING'S DIFFERENT THIS YEAR! I'LL HAVE TO PAY $300 FOR A WHOLE NEW SUIT!
NO; YOU WON'T.

NO??
CERTAINLY NOT.
Boutique

THIS YEAR YOU'LL HAVE TO PAY $300 FOR THE ACCESSORY!

A CAREER...
A RELATIONSHIP...
A FAMILY...

A WORKOUT PROGRAM...
A DIET PROGRAM...
A READING PROGRAM...
A SKIN CARE PROGRAM...
A HOME...
A SPORT...
A CAUSE...

I HAVE IT ALL.

AND I CARRY IT ALL WITH ME.
TOTE
GUISEWITE

WHY ARE YOU GETTING SO DRESSED UP JUST TO ORDER PIZZA WITH A GIRLFRIEND?
WHAT'S WRONG WITH LOOKING NICE FOR A GIRLFRIEND?

WHY NOT WEAR MY NICEST THINGS?? WHY NOT LET A ANOTHER WOMAN SEE JUST HOW STUNNING I CAN BE?!!

YOU LOOK GREAT, CATHY. I WISH I KNEW SOME SINGLE MEN TO FIX YOU UP WITH.
YOU DON'T KNOW ANY SINGLE MEN??

EXCUSE ME WHILE I GO CHANGE INTO SOME SWEATPANTS.
GUISEWITE

I BOUGHT A PAIR OF $110 BOOTS ON MY LUNCH HOUR. I FEEL SICK. HOW COULD I DO THAT TO MYSELF??
UP
DOWN

I HAVE TO MAKE MORE MONEY, THAT'S ALL THERE IS TO IT.... A RAISE.. NO. A BONUS! I MUST DO SOMETHING TO DESERVE A HUGE BONUS!
PRODUCT TESTING INC.
BOOTS

GIVE ME THE WORK. I WILL DO ALL THE WORK. BRING ME ALL YOUR WORK!
BOOTS

...AREN'T YOU GOING TO SAY ANYTHING, MR. PINKLEY??
LET ME KNOW WHEN SHE GOES COAT SHOPPING.
BOOTS
GUISEWITE

IT'S GORGEOUS! IT'S VERSATILE! IT'S A CLASSIC!

IT'S HOT! IT'S FABULOUS! IT'S SEXY! IT'S SMASHING! IT'S INCREDIBLE!

IT MAKES YOU LOOK LIKE A SCRAWNY TOOTHPICK.
SOLD!!

IF MOTHERS WERE ON COMMISSION, I'D BE A BILLIONAIRE.

DID YOU WANT TO TRY THAT?
NO. I JUST WANT TO LOOK.

THAT'S ADORABLE ON.
I'M JUST LOOKING.
WANT ME TO PUT THAT IN A ROOM FOR YOU?
NO. JUST LOOKING.

MAY I HOLD THAT?
I JUST WANT TO LOOK! WON'T YOU LEAVE ME ALONE SO I CAN JUST LOOK IN PEACE?!

OH, MISS... MISS?? MISS?!!
GO AHEAD. LOOK.

THERE'S NO MIRROR IN MY DRESSING ROOM.

DRESSING ROOM MIRRORS ARE FOR THE INSECURE. NONE OF THE TRENDIER BOUTIQUES HAVE THEM.

WOMEN TODAY LOOK AT OUR BODIES A WHOLE NEW WAY.

WHAT ARE YOU DOING IN THERE, CATHY?
I'M TRYING TO SEE MY REFLECTION IN THE TOP OF MY FELT-TIP PEN CAP.

IT'S ALMOST IMPOSSIBLE TO KNOW WHERE OUR OWN INSTINCTS LEAVE OFF AND PEER PRESSURE BEGINS, CHARLENE.
I KNOW, CATHY.
WHAT'S A NEED? WHAT'S JUST A TREND? SOMETIMES I WONDER IF THERE'S ANY DIFFERENCE AT ALL.
YEAH... YOU'RE STARTING TO WONDER IF YOU WANT A BABY JUST SO YOU'LL FIT IN?
WORSE. I'M HAVING A BIOLOGICAL URGE TO BUY CHUNKY SILVER JEWELRY.
I HATE RETURNING THINGS, MOM.
WE ALL HATE RETURNING THINGS, CATHY, BUT IT HAS TO BE DONE.
Boutique
I HATE FACING THE SALESPERSON. I NEVER KNOW WHAT TO SAY.
JUST TELL THE TRUTH.
SALE
HOT NEW
SALE
NEW
NEW
NEW
REASON FOR RETURN?
I WANTED AN EXCUSE TO GO SHOPPING AGAIN.
YOU'LL LET ME FIX YOU UP ON A BLIND DATE?!!
SHHH!!
CHARLENE
I THINK BLIND DATES ARE GREAT.
YOU DO?
ABSOLUTELY! IT MEANS YOU'RE FINALLY READY FOR A DATE THAT'S BEEN SELECTED BY SOMEONE WHO'S REALLY SENSITIVE TO YOUR NEEDS.
I'M READY FOR A DATE THAT I CAN BLAME ON SOMEONE ELSE.
CHARLENE

CHARLENE, BEFORE I LET YOU FIX ME UP, I WOULD NEED TO KNOW YOU'RE IN NO WAY SEEKING REVENGE FOR ANYONE I'VE FIXED **YOU** UP WITH BEFORE.
HOWARD, "THE HUMAN COMPUTER CHIP," IS FORGOTTEN, CATHY.
UH... I WOULD ALSO NEED TO KNOW THE INCIDENT WITH LOUIS IS FORGOTTEN.
LOUIS, "THE TRILINGUAL NUDIST," IS HISTORY.
PHONE
LIFE IS TOO SHORT TO SPEND IT SEEKING REVENGE FOR LOSERS LIKE THEM.
WELL, THANK YOU... THAT'S A RELIEF....
PHONE
CHARLENE
HOWEVER, I **WILL** BE GETTING EVEN FOR EDWARD, "THE KING OF TORTELLINI ALFREDO."
PHONE
CHARLENE
Guisewite

IF YOU HATE THE MAN I FIX YOU UP WITH, YOU WILL TURN THE HATRED BACK ON ME, AND IT WILL DESTROY OUR FRIENDSHIP, CATHY.
YES.

IF YOU LOVE HIM, YOU'LL START SPENDING ALL YOUR TIME WITH HIM, AND IT WILL DESTROY OUR FRIENDSHIP.
YES.

IF HE'S TOLERABLE, BUT NO ONE YOU'D EVER WANT TO SEE AGAIN, YOU'LL REALIZE I DON'T REALLY KNOW YOU AT ALL, AND IT WILL DESTROY OUR FRIENDSHIP.
YES.

TEMPTING, ISN'T IT?
HOW MANY CHANCES DO WE GET IN LIFE FOR SUCH A SURE THING?

YOU NEED PHYSICAL DESCRIPTIONS BEFORE YOU'LL MEET SOMEONE, CATHY? FINE... "RECEDING HAIRLINE, SQUINTY EYES, SMIRKS A LOT"....
BLEAH. FORGET HIM.

THAT WAS BRUCE WILLIS.
BRUCE?? WAIT.... BRUCE??
HOW ABOUT "SCRAWNY, BIG MOUTH, LIKES TO RIP HIS CLOTHES OFF"....

BLEAH. FORGET HIM.
THAT WAS MICK JAGGER. HOW ABOUT "REDDISH HAIR, CUTE FACE, ALWAYS SMILING"..

YES! I'LL TAKE HIM! YES!!
HOWDY DOODY.

THE DOWNFALL OF THE BLIND DATE IS THE AMOUNT OF TIME BETWEEN WHEN YOU HEAR ABOUT EACH OTHER AND WHEN YOU ACTUALLY MEET, CATHY.

GIVEN EVEN ONE DAY, SOME PEOPLE CAN CREATE A FANTASY SO GRAND, THE OTHER PERSON COULD NEVER MATCH UP. SOME CAN DO THE SAME DAMAGE IN ONE HOUR...

BUT WHAT IF YOU HAD NO TIME?? WHAT IF THERE WAS NOT EVEN ONE SECOND TO THINK BETWEEN.... TA DA! CATHY, MEET BURT!!

BLEAH.
YOU'RE PERFECT FOR EACH OTHER.

"BURT"? THAT'S A NICE NAME. "BURT"!
OH, NO, MOM. HE'S NOTHING! I SHOULDN'T HAVE MENTIONED HIM.

IS HE NICE? IS HE CUTE??
NO, MOM. FORGET HIM. NO! I WAS JUST MAKING CONVERSATION!

THINK HE'LL CALL??
MOM, HE'S GROSS. I WAS REPULSED BY HIM. I WOULD NEVER EVER EVER GO OUT WITH HIM!!

WHY DID YOU EVEN BRING HIM UP, CATHY?
I WANT MOM TO KNOW I'M KEEPING AN OPEN MIND TOWARDS MEETING NEW PEOPLE.

NOTHING RUINS A RELATIONSHIP FASTER THAN A DESPERATE WOMAN, CATHY.
I WON'T ACT DESPERATE, CHARLENE.

IT'S NOT JUST HOW YOU ACT. IT'S A LOOK IN YOUR EYE.
I WON'T HAVE THE LOOK.
IT'S A GESTURE... A NUANCE.
I WON'T GESTURE. NO NUANCES.

IT'S...
JUST FORGET IT! WHO NEEDS IT?!! JUST TAKE ALL THE MEN FOR YOURSELF, CHARLENE! I QUIT!!

ONE DOWN, 75 MILLION WOMEN TO GO...

CATHY, YOU SPENT ALL WEEKEND SHOPPING FOR A NEW DRESS FOR YOUR BLIND DATE..

...YOU SPENT YOUR LUNCH HOUR HUNTING FOR SHOES... FOUR HOURS DOING A FACIAL, MANICURE AND WORKOUT... AND NOW ANOTHER THREE HOURS OF PREENING....

...ALL THIS, AND YOU'RE JUST MEETING HIM FOR A CUP OF COFFEE??

I DON'T WANT TO WASTE THE WHOLE EVENING ON HIM IF WE DON'T LIKE EACH OTHER.

OH, NO. PLEASE DON'T LET THAT BE MY DATE. NO... PLEASE DON'T BE DEAN...

PLEASE...PLEASE.. GIVE ME A BREAK JUST THIS ONE TIME...PLEASE...
SANDRA?

NO! I'M NOT SANDRA! NO YOU'RE NOT DEAN?! NO!! I AM NOT SANDRA!!

THANK HEAVENS.

CATHY! HI! WHAT ARE YOU DOING HERE??
OH, HI...AHEM.. .. I'M JUST MEETING SOMEONE.

HE MUST REALLY BE SPECIAL. YOU LOOK GREAT!
OH, NO...UM... NO. NO, HE'S JUST A FRIEND.

NO ONE LOOKS LIKE THAT FOR JUST A FRIEND! THIS IS SOMEONE SPECIAL! VERY, VERY SPECIAL...
ARE EITHER OF YOU NAMED CATHY?

....OR ELSE IT'S A BLIND DATE!
WHERE IS THE LADIES ROOM AND DOES IT HAVE A WINDOW I CAN LEAP OUT OF?

SHORTLY AFTER MEETING, THE PERSON WHO'S MORE ATTRACTED TO THE OTHER WILL DO SOMETHING GOOFY, THUS ESTABLISHING THE POWER STRUCTURE OF THE COUPLE.
DEAN?
CATHY?

KNOWING THIS, ASTUTE SINGLES TRY HARD TO REMAIN COOL SO THE OTHER CAN MAKE THE FIRST BLUNDER.

WHILE A TOTAL "COOLNESS STANDOFF" IS USUALLY A SIGN OF GENUINE, EQUAL DISINTEREST, A THIRD PARTY CAN SOMETIMES BREAK THROUGH TO AN EVEN MORE RARE PHENOMENON:
MENUS?

THE MIRACLE OF MUTUAL ATTRACTION.
GLEEZEEP.

WHAT'S YOUR GENERAL ORIENTATION TOWARD LIFE, DEAN?
HUH?
WHAT'S YOUR BASIC NATURE? WHAT DO YOU RESPOND TO?
HUH?
WHAT'S THE ESSENCE OF YOUR PERSONALITY AND RELATIONSHIP TO OTHERS?
HUH?
IT'D BE SO MUCH EASIER IF I COULD JUST ASK WHAT HIS SIGN IS....

CHARLENE, MY BLIND DATE WAS...
I'M SORRY. HE USED TO BE CUTER! HE USED TO BE NICER!
NO, WAIT! I HAD A GREAT TIME!
IT'S NOT MY FAULT! I HAVEN'T SEEN HIM! I'M INNOCENT!!
WE'RE CRAZY ABOUT EACH OTHER.
YOU'RE CRAZY ABOUT EACH OTHER??
WAIT! NOT THAT CRAZY! JUST OK! FAIR! SO-SO.
I KNEW HIM FIRST! I WANT HIM BACK! I HAVE DIBS!

PERSON GREETING A BLINKING LIGHT, INDICATING THERE ARE MESSAGES:
"Blink" Blink Blink
PERSON GREETING A SOLID, STUNNED BEAM OF LIGHT, INDICATING NO MESSAGES:
PERSON GREETING NO LIGHT AT ALL, INDICATING SHE FORGOT TO TURN THE MACHINE ON.
THOSE OF US WHO DON'T LOOK LIKE OUR PETS ARE STARTING TO LOOK LIKE OUR ANSWERING MACHINES.

THERE'S NO REASON A WOMAN CAN'T CALL A MAN AFTER THE FIRST DATE, CATHY.
SURE... I COULD HAVE CALLED RIGHT AFTER THE DATE, BUT HE SPECIFICALLY SAID HE WANTED TO CALL ME.

BY THE TIME I WAITED LONG ENOUGH TO GIVE HIM A CHANCE TO CALL, IT WAS TOO LATE TO CALL HIM WITHOUT SEEMING TO BE ASKING WHAT HAPPENED.

NOW I CAN'T CALL HIM. HE'LL KNOW I'VE BEEN WAITING. I'LL SOUND TOO ANXIOUS. TOO NEEDY. NO. BEFORE WOULD HAVE BEEN PERFECT. NOW WOULD BE HUMILIATING. AACK. NO. IT'S TOO LATE. NO.

HOW LONG HAS IT BEEN?
THIRTY-SIX HOURS.
COFFEE ROOM RU
Guisewite

THIS BOOK SAYS THE WAY TO A MAN'S HEART IS TO LEARN TO SPEAK IN HIS "VISUAL, AUDITORY, OR FEELINGS-RELATED LOVE LANGUAGE," CATHY.

THIS BOOK SAYS MEN CAN'T RESIST A WOMAN WHO'S MASTERED THE "CRITICISM-PRAISE BALANCE"... THIS ONE SAYS YOU CAN MAKE THEM GO CRAZY WITH "THE FIVE KEYS TO ROMANTIC TENSION"....

CALL ME, DEAN! CALL ME! CALL ME! CALL ME!!
SMASH

THEY ALL KIND OF RUN TOGETHER WHEN YOU TRY TO PUT THEM INTO PRACTICE.
Guisewite

HE SAID HE'D CALL. HE NEVER CALLED. WHY? ONE BRAVE WOMAN GOES IN SEARCH OF THE ANSWER.

DID HE NEVER MEAN TO CALL AT ALL? DID HE MEAN TO CALL BUT CHANGE HIS MIND? ...HER MIND RACES, TRYING TO FUSE QUESTIONS WITH A CLEAR ARTICULATION OF JUST HOW MISERABLE THIS MAKES A WOMAN FEEL.

SHE STRUGGLES TO STAY COOL... COOL BUT THOROUGH... THOROUGH BUT INTENSE... REMEMBER ALL THE QUESTIONS... EXPRESS THE FEELINGS... KEEP THE DIGNITY... HER HEART FILLS... HER BRAIN IS POUNDING... SHE REACHES THE DOOR...

PBLTTT!
AACK!
...THE DIALOGUE BEGINS.

IT DOESN'T BOTHER YOU THAT I WENT OUT WITH SOMEONE, IRVING?
YOU SAID YOU WEREN'T SEEING HIM AGAIN. IS HE STILL CALLING?
NO, I'M NOT SEEING HIM OR TALKING TO HIM.
DO YOU WISH YOU WERE WITH HIM?
NO. I DON'T WANT TO SEE HIM, TALK TO HIM OR BE WITH HIM, BUT IF HE'D TURNED OUT TO BE SOMEONE ELSE, I MIGHT HAVE WANTED TO THINK ABOUT IT!!
...WHAT DOES IT TAKE TO MAKE A MAN JEALOUS ANYMORE?...

WHAT'S CATHY DOING TONIGHT?
SHE MENTIONED PAYING A SURPRISE VISIT ON HER DATE FROM LAST WEEKEND.

IMAGINE! IN MY DAY, A WOMAN WHO HADN'T HEARD FROM A MAN ALL WEEK WOULD NEVER BE ABLE TO CALL OR VISIT HIM!

ISN'T IT WONDERFUL THAT WOMEN TODAY CAN REALLY GO AFTER WHAT THEY WANT IN A RELATIONSHIP ??!

OPEN THIS DOOR YOU COWARD!!
BAM
BAM
BAM

I WAS GOING TO CALL!
I TRIED TO CALL!
I LOST YOUR NUMBER!
I FORGOT YOUR LAST NAME!
YOUR LINE WAS BUSY!
MY PHONE IS BROKEN!
YOUR PHONE IS BROKEN!
YOUR ANSWERING MACHINE IS BROKEN!

I'VE BEEN SICK!
I HAD A WORK CRISIS!
A FAMILY CRISIS!
A NATURAL DISASTER!
I'VE BEEN OUT OF TOWN!
I WAS INTIMIDATED!
I WAS CONFUSED!
AN OLD GIRLFRIEND RESURFACED!

...(pant, pant) ANYTHING ?? ANYTHING AT ALL? (pant, pant)....
NOT EVEN CLOSE.

MY MOTHER IS VISITING!
MY GRANDMOTHER IS VISITING!
I WAS BEING COY!
MY APARTMENT FLOODED!
I HAD DENTAL SURGERY!
I WAS ROBBED!
I HAD FOOD POISONING!
I'M BEING TRANSFERRED!
I'VE HAD AMNESIA!
I LOST MY HOUSE KEYS!

WHY WAS IT MY JOB TO CALL CATHY? MEN WOULD LOVE IT IF A WOMAN CALLED.

OH, SURE, MEN SAY THAT... BUT THEN WHEN THE WOMAN CALLS YOU THINK SHE'S EASY ...SHE'S NEEDY... SHE'S DESPERATE...

THE VERY MOMENT YOU KNOW SHE'S MOST VULNERABLE, YOU ACCUSE HER OF BEING TOO AGGRESSIVE... RETREAT INTO YOUR SHELL ...AND THEN BLAME THE WHOLE RELATIONSHIP ON HER!

THOSE ARE ALL THE THINGS WE LOVE.

...WELL, THANKS. YOU MADE ME REALLY SEE HOW A WOMAN CAN FEEL WHEN A MAN SAYS HE'LL CALL AND THEN DOESN'T, CATHY.
YEAH... WELL, YOU REMINDED ME THAT MEN CAN BE INSECURE, TOO.
WHEN A WOMAN GIVES ME HER PHONE NUMBER LIKE THIS, I WILL NEVER AGAIN JUST STUFF IT IN A DRAWER!
AND I WON'T WAIT FOR THE MAN TO TAKE ACTION!
SO...UM... I'LL CALL YOU, CATHY..
AND I'LL CALL YOU, DEAN.
Rip Rip Rip
Rip Rip Rip Rip
Guisewite

A ROOF OVER OUR HEADS... A SAFE PLACE TO SLEEP... WARM CLOTHES TO WEAR... HOPE FOR THE FUTURE...

WHEN YOU HAVE A TINY NEW BABY LIKE ZENITH, YOU REALIZE IT ISN'T ENOUGH TO JUST GIVE THANKS FOR THE FOOD ON THE TABLE.

SPLASH
PLOP
WHEE
SPLAT
BAM BAM

NOW WE GIVE THANKS FOR THE FOOD UNDER THE TABLE.
Guisewite

WHEN THANKSGIVING IS OVER, IT REALLY SEEMS AS IF WINTER HAS BEGUN.

THE AIR IS COLD, THE FIRST SNOW FALLS...

AND EVERYWHERE YOU GO, YOU START HEARING THOSE FAMILIAR WORDS....

AAACK! MY $100 BOOTS ARE GETTING WET!!!
MALL
LOT A
MALL
Guisewite

AREN'T YOU GOING TO DO ALL YOUR CHRISTMAS SHOPPING BY CATALOGUE THIS YEAR, CATHY ?
NO.
IT'S SO EFFICIENT!
GIFTS
ANDREA, DON'T YOU THINK YOU'RE MISSING THE WHOLE POINT ?...THE WHOLE MAGICAL EXPERIENCE OF GOING OUT SHOPPING FOR YOUR LOVED ONES ??!
WHY ? BECAUSE I CAN'T TOUCH THE GIFTS I PICK OUT FOR PEOPLE ?
YOU CAN'T TRY ON ANY CLOTHES.

HOW COULD YOU BLAB MY BLIND DATE STORY TO THE WHOLE BUILDING, CHARLENE ??
I DON'T KNOW, CATHY.
RECEPTIONIST
I PRIDE MYSELF IN MY ABILITY TO RECEIVE AND DISTRIBUTE INFORMATION, BUT THIS ONE WENT OVER THE TOP.
I WHISPERED IT... HONED IT... ROUTED IT!... PEOPLE DON'T JUST KNOW THE STORY.. ...BY 9:30 THIS MORNING MOST OF THE OFFICE COULD RE-ENACT YOUR ENTIRE LAST CONVERSATION !!!
I DON'T THINK CATHY MEANT IT AS A COMPLIMENT, CHARLENE.
OH.
RECEPTIONIST

WHAT'S IRVING BEEN DOING WHILE YOU'VE BEEN WORRYING ABOUT DEAN, CATHY ?
I WISH I KNEW.
POPCORN
DOES HE GET CRAZY WITH JEALOUSY ? DOES HE SNEAK AROUND WITH OTHER PEOPLE WHEN I SNEAK AROUND WITH OTHER PEOPLE ? HOW WOULD I EVER FIND OUT ??
POPCORN
THIS IS THE ONE THING MY RELATIONSHIP WITH IRVING HAS ALWAYS BEEN LACKING.
TRUST ?
SPIES.

I CAN'T THINK OF ANYTHING TO GET FOR THE MEN ON MY LIST.
Gift Center

GO THROUGH WOMEN'S PERFUME, WOMEN'S COSMETICS, WOMEN'S JEWELRY, WOMEN'S PURSES, WOMEN'S HOSIERY, WOMEN'S HATS, WOMEN'S LUGGAGE, WOMEN'S BARRETTES, WOMEN'S SUNGLASSES, WOMEN'S SHOES, WOMEN'S BELTS, WOMEN'S LINGERIE, WOMEN'S SPORTSWEAR, WOMEN'S FORMAL WEAR AND YOU'LL SEE A LITTLE CORNER FOR THE MEN.

YOU HAVE 50 DEPARTMENTS FOR WOMEN AND ONE LITTLE CORNER FOR MEN ??
Gift Center

WE COULDN'T THINK OF ANYTHING, EITHER.

THIS 21-RANGE ANALOG TESTER MAKES A GREAT GIFT FOR THAT SPECIAL GUY!
THAT MAKES A GREAT GIFT??
FOR HIM

THE 7-BAND EQUALIZER WITH 80-WATT BOOSTER IS ON SO MANY WISH LISTS!
YOU'RE KIDDING.

AND WHAT MAN DOESN'T DREAM OF OWNING A 5-TIER TACKLE BOX WITH DETACHABLE WORM BASKET?!!

DID YOU GET MY CHRISTMAS PRESENT?
ONCE I FOUND OUT WHAT YOU'D WANT I DIDN'T LIKE YOU ANYMORE.

I'LL COME TO STAY AT YOUR HOUSE ON THE 23RD AND WILL LEAVE ON THE 26TH, MOM.
OH. SO SOON? YOU CAN'T STAY LONGER?
CATHY

I'M NOT EVEN THERE YET!
YOUR VISITS ARE ALWAYS SO SHORT.
CATH

MOM, YOU HAVE THREE WEEKS BEFORE I GET THERE. ...WE'LL TALK TWICE A DAY.. ...ARE YOU GOING TO DO THIS TO ME FORTY-TWO MORE TIMES BEFORE THE HOLIDAY BEGINS?!!

WHY SAVE IT ALL FOR CHRISTMAS WHEN I HAVE THIS MUCH TO GIVE?
DEC

YOU DIDN'T BUY PAUL SIMON'S NEW "GRACELAND" ALBUM YET, DID YOU, IRVING?
PAUL SIMON · GRACELAND
NO...GREAT! HERE IT IS! I'LL TAKE IT!
PAUL SIMON · GRACELAND
WITH CHRISTMAS THIS CLOSE, YOU WOULDN'T HAVE GOTTEN...
THE SPRINGSTEEN SET! GREAT! I'LL TAKE IT...AND ISN'T THAT THE NEW...
AAACK!
SPRINGSTEEN LIVE
MAY I HELP YOU?
MAKE MY BOYFRIEND GO HOME WHILE THERE'S STILL SOMETHING LEFT THAT HE DOESN'T OWN.
SPRING
NEW
Groening

WHEN EVERYONE USED TO GO OUT WITH EVERYONE, THE "PERFECT GIFT" WAS A $5 ALBUM.
MAL
THEN THE $100 WALKMAN BECAME THE "PERFECT GIFT"... PEOPLE STARTED DATING FEWER PEOPLE.
THEN THE $300 CD PLAYER BECAME THE "PERFECT GIFT." PEOPLE GOT MONOGAMOUS.
Holiday Specials
THIS YEAR THE PERFECT GIFT IS A $4,000 AUDIO-VIDEO HOME ELECTRONICS CENTER!
TIME TO BREAK UP.
Groening

PERFECT SOUND. MEN LOVE IT! MEN LUST FOR IT! LOOK! THIS REMOTE CD PLAYER HAS A 95db SIGNAL-TO-NOISE RATIO, 95db DYNAMIC RANGE, 5hz TO 20,000hz FREQUENCY RESPONSE AND HARMONIC DISTORTION OF JUST 0.003%!!
THIS BABY TAKES BASS TO 26hz WITH A SUB-BASS ACOUSTIC SUSPENSION DRIVER!! FRONT-MOUNTED EXPONENTIAL TWEETERS BLAST TO 21,500hz! A 38mm VOICE COIL GOES TO 200°c!! AND SHE'S FUSE-PROTECTED TO 200 WATTS PEAK!
GIFTS
IT'S ENDLESS! SMASH THE CYMBALS AT 16,000hz! BLOW OUT THE SAX AT 19,500! 20 EQUALIZER CONTROLS! TEN VU METERS! AUDIO ECSTASY! REVERB ONE NOTE INTO A 3-D EXPLOSION OF PURE, PERFECT, DIGITAL SOUND!!
DO YOU HAVE ANYTHING THAT WILL MAKE MY BOYFRIEND LISTEN TO ME?
CAN YOU PLAY KEYBOARD?
SAVE
Groening

WHAT HAPPENED TO YOUR BIG PLAN TO START DOING NAUTILUS AGAIN, CATHY?
WHAT HAPPENED TO YOUR ROWING MACHINE, IRVING?
WHAT ABOUT THE DAILY 5-MILE RUN?
WHAT ABOUT THE ROWING MACHINE?
THE STATIONARY BIKE?
THE ROWING MACHINE?
AEROBICS CLASS?
ROWING MACHINE?
WEIGHTS?
ROWING MACHINE?
ALL RIGHT! YOU WIN! FORGET I BROUGHT IT UP!!
USED PROPERLY, ONE ROWING MACHINE CAN DO THE WORK OF A WHOLE GYM.
Guisewite

WELL, I SEE THE McPHERSONS HAVE GONE TO COMPUTERIZED ADDRESS LABELS ON THEIR PRE-PRINTED CHRISTMAS CARDS.

SO WHAT, MOM? IT JUST MEANS THEY HAVE A COMPUTER THIS YEAR.

CATHY, THE USE OF COMPUTERIZED ADDRESS LABELS SAYS MUCH MORE THAN "WE HAVE A COMPUTER"!

IT SAYS, "WE HAVE A COMPUTER AND SOMEONE IN OUR FAMILY UNDERSTOOD THE INSTRUCTION BOOK."
SHOW-OFFS!

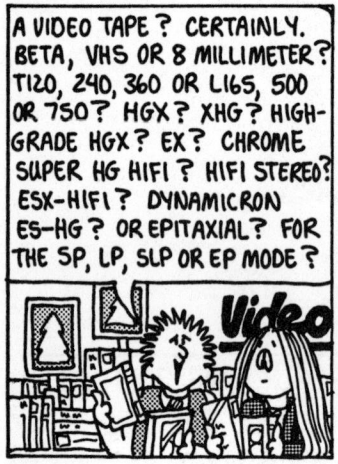
A VIDEO TAPE? CERTAINLY. BETA, VHS OR 8 MILLIMETER? T120, 240, 360 OR L165, 500 OR 750? HGX? XHG? HIGH-GRADE HGX? EX? CHROME SUPER HG HIFI? HIFI STEREO? ESX-HIFI? DYNAMICRON ES-HG? OR EPITAXIAL? FOR THE SP, LP, SLP OR EP MODE?
Video

MAYBE I'LL JUST GET AN AUDIO TAPE.
Video

CERTAINLY. HIGH BIAS, NORMAL BIAS OR METAL? 46, 90 OR 60? TDK SA-X, AD-S, D, SA, MA-X OR HX-S ??? SONY HF, HF-S, UX-S, UX-PRO, METAL-ES, UCX-60 OR LH-MAXIMA? BASF LH OR CHROMDIOXID EXTRA II? MAXELL XL II-S, UDS-II, XL I-S, OR MX-METAXIAL POSITION IEC, TYPE IV,? UDS-I, XL-I, XL-II, UXHG
Audio

IT'S FINALLY HAPPENED... I CAN'T EVEN FIGURE OUT HOW TO BUY SOMETHING THAT'S TOTALLY BLANK.
Audio/Video
Holiday

"MERRY CHRISTMAS, BARB! HERE'S A LITTLE SOMETHING I GOT FOR..."..NO. TOO DEMEANING. "A BOX FOR BARB!.. HA, HA..."..NO. TOO GOOFY.
Holiday Cards

"THINKING OF YOU, BARB..".. NO. TOO NORMAL. "MY DEAREST BARB..".. TOO MUSHY.
Merry Christmas!

"HI, BARB!"... NO. "FRIEND BARB...". NO. "HERE'S TO..." ...NO. "MERRIEST WI.." NO.
RIP
RIP
RIP
RIP

"DEAR BARB, THERE WILL BE NO GIFT THIS YEAR. I USED UP MY WHOLE BOX OF CARDS ON YOU."

WHERE'S THE ACCOUNTING DEPARTMENT, CATHY?
THEY FIGURED NO ONE WOULD GET ANYTHING DONE SO THEY WENT HOME EARLY FOR CHRISTMAS.
CHRISTMAS IS STILL TEN DAYS AWAY!
YEAH... IT CREEPS UP EVERY YEAR.
PEOPLE USED TO START LEAVING EARLY ON CHRISTMAS EVE... THEN AT NOON ON THE 23RD... THEN AT 3:00 ON THE 22ND... AND NOW...
I'M GOING TO SPEAK TO THE MANAGEMENT SQUAD ABOUT THIS!!
THE MANAGEMENT SQUAD NEVER CAME BACK FROM THANKSGIVING.

"TO BOB AND SUE"... WHAT HAVE THEY BEEN UP TO, CATHY?
WHO KNOWS, ANDREA?
THE ONLY TIME BOB AND SUE EVER THINK ABOUT ME IS WHEN THEY SEE MY NAME ON THEIR CHRISTMAS CARD LIST AND WONDER IF THIS IS THE YEAR TO CROSS ME OFF.
WHY WOULD YOU KEEP SENDING CHRISTMAS CARDS TO PEOPLE LIKE THAT??!
WE HAVE A LOT IN COMMON.

MAYBE I SHOULD JUST READ MY LIST AND YOU CAN HELP ME DECIDE, CATHY.
OK.
GIFTS
GUESS JEANS... REEBOK SNEAKERS... PERUVIAN HAND-LOOMED CAPE... OVERSIZED DENIM JACKET WITH EMBROIDERED INLAYS... ONYX STUD EARRINGS... ITALIAN LEATHER JUMPSUIT... PICTURE BOOK OF SOUTHWEST AMERICAN POTTERY....
OH, ANDREA! ANYTHING!! I WOULD LOVE ANY OF THOSE THINGS!!!
THIS IS THE LIST FOR OUR SIX-MONTH-OLD DAUGHTER.
OH.
WE HAVE YOU DOWN FOR A FRUITCAKE.
NOUVEAU BABY SHOPPE
OPEN

OF COURSE, ALL TOYS FOR MY BABY MUST BE 100% SAFE, TESTED AND WHOLESOME.
OF COURSE.
TOYS

THEY MUST BE NON-TOXIC, NON-POLLUTING, NON-FLAMMABLE, NON-VIOLENT, STERILE, AND VACUUM SEALED IN THE ORIGINAL CARTON WITH A CLEAR LIST OF MATERIALS PRINTED ON THE BOX !!

YOUR GERM-FREE DAUGHTER IS SUCKING DIRT OFF THE CAR KEYS YOU DUG OUT OF THE BOTTOM OF YOUR PURSE AND THEN DROPPED ON THE FLOOR, ANDREA.

WHAT DO YOU HAVE THAT'S FAIRLY CLEAN?
TOYS

"TRANSFORMER" TOYS ARE A VERY HOT ITEM! FOR LITTLE BOYS WE HAVE BATTLE TANKS THAT TRANSFORM INTO DEATH RAY LASER GUNS...BOMBER JETS THAT TRANSFORM INTO MINI-NUCLEAR WARHEADS....
TOYS
ATTACK

...AND FOR LITTLE GIRLS WE HAVE KITCHENETTES THAT TRANSFORM INTO MAKEUP TRAYS!

YOUR "BOY TOYS" TRANSFORM INTO MURDER WEAPONS AND YOUR "GIRL TOYS" TRANSFORM INTO BEAUTY PRODUCTS?? ARE YOU OUT OF YOUR MINDS?! HAVE YOU TOTALLY LOST TOUCH?

MY CUSTOMER IS TRANSFORMING INTO A MONSTER.
NO BIGGIE. JUST TRANSFORM YOURSELF INTO A ROBOT.
BAM BAM BAM

WHAT DO YOU MEAN IT'S TOO LATE TO ORDER FROM A CATALOG FOR CHRISTMAS?? THIS IS THE UNITED STATES OF AMERICA!

FEDERAL EXPRESS IT! EXPRESS MAIL! EMERY! AIRBORNE! BLUE LABEL UPS! ZAP MAIL! SATELLITE TRANSMISSION!!

CHARTER A JET! HIRE A MESSENGER! BUT GET THAT PACKAGE DELIVERED BEFORE CHRISTMAS EVE !!!

THE '80s GIFT: A $15 WATCH WITH A $150 SHIPPING CHARGE.

MY BOYFRIEND HAS 4 WATCHES, 4 TELEPHONES, 6 RADIOS, 3 TV SETS, 5 TAPE PLAYERS, 4 CAMERAS...
GIFTS
...8 CALCULATORS, 10 KEY RINGS, 12 MUGS, 6 SWEATSUITS, 5 PAIRS OF SUNGLASSES, 43 NECKTIES, AND 7,000 SHIRTS.
GIFTS
GIFTS
SWEATS
for HIM
I'VE QUIT LOOKING FOR SOMETHING UNIQUE AND AM TRYING TO FIND SOMETHING HE HAS LESS THAN THREE OF.

A SHIRT FOR DAD... SWEATER FOR MOM... GLOVES FOR ANDREA... A CAMERA..TOTE-BAG... WORKOUT TAPE... NECKLACE... WALLET... PHONE ... BOOK... ALBUM... COFFEE MAKER... STOCKING STUFFERS ... TABLE DECORATIONS....
...OK. A SHIRT FOR DAD... A SWEATER FOR MOM...
...OK, A PARKING SPACE. JUST GIVE ME A PARKING SPACE. ALL I WANT IS A PARKING SPACE!!
AS A RELATIONSHIP GOES ON, OUR EXPECTATIONS GET MORE REALISTIC.

WANT TO SEE WHAT I GOT IRVING FOR CHRISTMAS?
NO. IT'S ALL WRAPPED.
I DON'T MIND OPENING IT.
DON'T BE SILLY.
DON'T YOU WANT TO LOOK AT IT??
CATHY, GET HOLD OF YOURSELF!!
YOU'RE RIGHT. WITH ALL I HAVE TO DO, IT WOULD BE CRAZY TO STAND HERE WITH YOU AND UNWRAP THE ONE GIFT I HAVE READY!
...WHEN I CAN WAIT UNTIL YOU LEAVE AND DO IT IN PEACE.
RIP
RIP
RIP
RIP
RIP
RIP

I WANT THIS TO BE OUR BEST HOLIDAY VISIT EVER, CATHY!
ME TOO, MOM!

I'VE THOUGHT OF ALL THE THINGS THAT ANNOY YOU AND HAVE PLEDGED NOT TO DO ANY OF THEM!
ME TOO!

HERE! IT'S ALL OUTLINED IN THIS ARTICLE ON COPING WITH HOLIDAY STRESS THAT I CLIPPED FOR YOU!

AACK!
AHAH!
THERE'S NOTHING LIKE THE FAMILIAR SOUNDS OF CHRISTMAS.

MERRY CHRISTMAS, CATHY. SHOULD I OPEN MINE FIRST?
NO.

I'LL OPEN MINE FIRST AND THEN IF WHAT I GOT YOU IS INAPPROPRIATE, I'LL RUN OUT TO THE STORE AND EXCHANGE IT AND RUN BACK WITH SOMETHING ELSE!

OH, HA, HA! THAT'S A GOOD ONE... BUT I'LL BET SOME PEOPLE ACTUALLY THINK LIKE THAT!!

STAY RIGHT WHERE YOU ARE.

YOU LOOK UPSET, CATHY. HERE. HAVE SOME NUTBREAD.
IF SOMETHING'S ON YOUR MIND, WHY DON'T YOU HAVE THE NUTBREAD, MOM?

I THINK SOMETHING'S BOTHERING YOUR FATHER. HE NEEDS THE NUTBREAD TREATMENT.
WANT SOME NUTBREAD, DAD??

WELL, OK... A LITTLE NUTBREAD NEVER HURT.
MAYBE JUST A TASTE.
NOTHING SMOOTHS THINGS OVER LIKE A FAT SLICE OF NUTBREAD!
CHOMP CHOMP
EAT CHOMP
EAT EAT

WHY CAN'T WE JUST SCREAM AT EACH OTHER LIKE NORMAL FAMILIES?

IRVING, I'VE BEEN SHOPPING ALL AFTERNOON AND I HAVE A SEXY LITTLE VALENTINE OUTFIT TO SHOW YOU...
AACK. I CAN'T BELIEVE I DID THAT... AACK! NOW HE'S COMING OVER!!
HE CAN'T SEE ME LIKE THIS! I LOOK RIDICULOUS! I LOOK LIKE A BIMBO! WHAT WAS I THINKING???
I DON'T SEE ANYTHING DIFFERENT, CATHY.
MEN HAVE NO IMAGINATION.
Guisewite

IF I EAT THIS PIECE OF CAKE, WILL I STILL BE ABLE TO GET INTO MY NEW YEAR'S EVE DRESS?? NO. CAKE TURNS INTO FAT ALMOST IMMEDIATELY.

HOWEVER, LIQUID CALORIES FLOAT AROUND BEFORE SETTLING INTO FAT.

I COULD STILL HAVE EGG-NOG... ICE CREAM... LIQUEFIED MOUSSE... AND ANY AMOUNT OF CHOLESTEROL SAUCE WITHOUT IT SHOWING UP ON ME BEFORE JANUARY 1!
ICE CREAM
EGG NOG

I'M DEFERRING MY GAINS UNTIL AFTER THE NEW YEAR.
ICE CREAM

"HOW TO WORK THE OFFICE HOLIDAY PARTY:
1. READ THE ROOM
2. MANEUVER YOURSELF TOWARD MAJOR CLIENTS AND KEY PERSONNEL..."

"3. MAXIMIZE EACH ENCOUNTER WITH BRIGHT, GOAL-ORIENTED CHITCHAT.
4. KEEP DIALOGUES BRIEF, SINCERE AND DIGNIFIED."

PARTY

"5. ARRIVE BEFORE PEOPLE HAVE HAD MORE THAN THREE DRINKS."

THEY FILLED THE WORLD WITH WORKOUT TAPES AND THEN PUT A CHOCOLATE CHIP COOKIE STAND ON EVERY CORNER...
1986
YEAR END ISSUE

THEY CHEERED US TO THE PEAK OF OUR CAREERS AND THEN SAID WE HAVE TEN MINUTES TO START HAVING CHILDREN... THEY MELLOWED US INTO MORE REALISTIC GOALS AND THEN SHOWED US A WOMAN WITH A 41" REAR GET MARRIED TO A PRINCE... THEY SAID WE COULD HAVE IT ALL, AND THEN CHARGED $200 FOR BOOTS.

NOW - OVERWEIGHT, CONFUSED, BROKE AND FRAZZLED - THEY'VE ANNOUNCED THAT IF WE'RE REALLY RESPONSIBLE, WE'LL SPEND OUR LAST SHRED OF MONEY ON SOMETHING HUGE TODAY SO WE CAN DEDUCT THE SALES TAX.

WELL, I GUESS WE KNOW WHAT TO SAY ABOUT THE END OF THIS YEAR!
IT WAS JUST GETTING GOOD!!

YOU ALREADY CHEATED ON YOUR DIET, DIDN'T YOU, CATHY?
I DID NOT.

YOU CONVINCED YOURSELF THAT ALL FOOD BOUGHT BEFORE MIDNIGHT LAST NIGHT IS "LAST YEAR'S FOOD" AND SO DOESN'T COUNT IF YOU EAT IT TODAY.

YOU RATIONALIZED THAT THE LEFTOVER NUTBREAD WAS A SOURCE OF PROTEIN AND THAT THE CHRISTMAS COOKIES WERE "FIBER"!

HOW CAN SOMEONE SO FAT BE SO TRANSPARENT?
Guisewite

8:00AM: BEGIN 1987 DIET.
8:02AM: RE-WRITE LIST OF DIET GOALS.

8:03AM: LOOK AT "FAT PHOTO"... LOOK AT BATHING SUIT... JOG... MEDITATE... RE-READ ENCOURAGING TESTIMONIALS... NOTE FEELINGS IN DIET DIARY... RECITE GOALS ALOUD... VISUALIZE..ACTUALIZE.. HYPNOTIZE AND....

CHOMP

8:04 AM: BEGIN 1987 DIET II.
Guisewite

I'VE EATEN BECAUSE I WAS FRUSTRATED, NERVOUS, ANGRY, EXCITED, LONELY, DEPRESSED, JEALOUS, HURT, HAPPY, DISCOURAGED, FAT, BROKE, INSECURE, EUPHORIC, CONTENT AND CONFUSED.

NOW I HAVE A DIET DIARY.
Diet Diary

IT'S FORCING ME TO RECOGNIZE AN ENTIRELY DIFFERENT MOTIVATION.

NOW I'M EATING SO I'LL HAVE SOMETHING TO WRITE DOWN IN MY CUTE NOTEBOOK.
Guisewite

THE PROFESSIONAL BUSINESS-PERSON: MENTALLY PSYCHED ...DEFENSES PRIMED...MUSCLES TENSED...NEGOTIATING SKILLS POISED LIKE LASERS AT THIS, HER FIRST ASTOUNDING CHALLENGE OF THE YEAR...
EEEEEY
YAAAH!!!
DONUTS
...GETTING IN AND OUT OF THE COFFEE ROOM WITHOUT TOUCHING A DONUT.
DONUTS

I WANT TO HAVE A "BEFORE" PICTURE OF ME LOOKING AS FAT AS POSSIBLE IN A LEOTARD FOR MY DIET DIARY, BUT AM TOO EMBARRASSED TO HAVE SOMEONE TAKE IT.
I FINALLY TAKE IT MYSELF IN A MIRROR, BUT AM TOO EMBARRASSED TO GET THE FILM DEVELOPED... I FINALLY GET THE FILM DEVELOPED, BUT AM TOO EMBARRASSED TO PICK IT UP...
AS A PHOTO LAB FULL OF STRANGERS STARE AT MY "FAT PICTURES," I SLOWLY ACCEPT THE ONE HIDEOUS CHOICE I HAVE....
...WHY CAN'T SHE JUST BEG ME TO RETURN THINGS LIKE OTHER DAUGHTERS?
ONE HOUR PHOTO

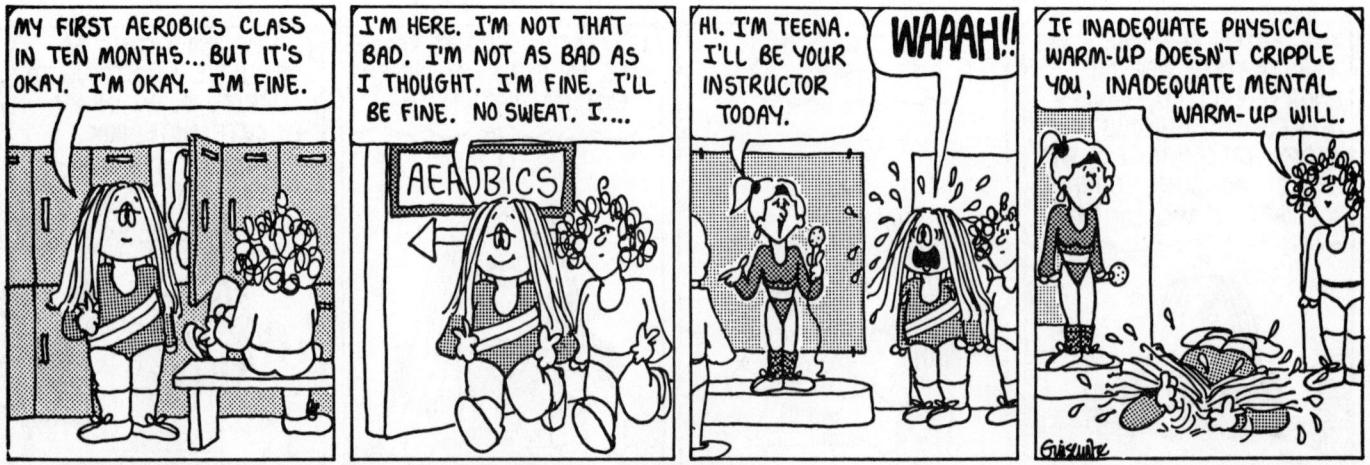
MY FIRST AEROBICS CLASS IN TEN MONTHS...BUT IT'S OKAY. I'M OKAY. I'M FINE.
I'M HERE. I'M NOT THAT BAD. I'M NOT AS BAD AS I THOUGHT. I'M FINE. I'LL BE FINE. NO SWEAT. I....
AEROBICS
HI. I'M TEENA. I'LL BE YOUR INSTRUCTOR TODAY.
WAAAH!!
IF INADEQUATE PHYSICAL WARM-UP DOESN'T CRIPPLE YOU, INADEQUATE MENTAL WARM-UP WILL.

THE PRE-PACKAGED DESSERT SNACK: ARTIFICIAL FLAVOR... FAKE COLOR... 17 CHEMICALS...

THE GOURMET COOKIE: PURE FRESH CREAM... IMPORTED CHOCOLATE... HAND-GROUND ORGANIC FLOUR... FRESH WHOLE SWEET BUTTER....

FOR THE 1987 DIETER, ANOTHER IMPOSSIBLE QUESTION:

WILL THE FAT STAY WITH ME LONGER IF IT'S MADE OF PRESERVATIVES OR IF IT'S MADE OF QUALITY INGREDIENTS?

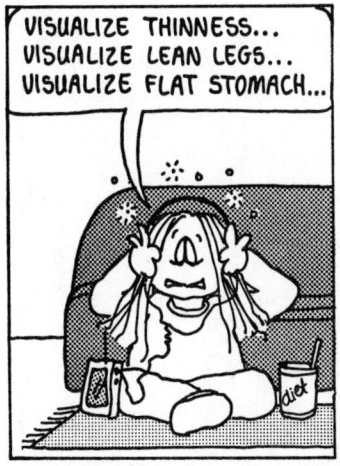
VISUALIZE THINNESS... VISUALIZE LEAN LEGS... VISUALIZE FLAT STOMACH...

VISUALIZE HOW MY HIPS WOULD HAVE LOOKED IF I'D GONE TO THE HEALTH CLUB FOR THE LAST TEN MONTHS....

DO YOU REALLY THINK THAT DOES ANY GOOD, CATHY?

IT'S 25 SECONDS WHEN I HAVEN'T EATEN ANYTHING.

SUGAR?
OH, NO. I USE ONLY ARTIFICIAL SWEETENER NOW.

I USE ARTIFICIAL SWEETENER, AND SO AM ALLOWED ONE TINY CORNER OF A BLUEBERRY MUFFIN...

...A TASTE OF CROISSANT... A SPEC OF LEFTOVER FRUITCAKE... A BITE OF TURNOVER... A TOUCH OF DANISH...

AN OUNCE OF PREVENTION IS WORTH A POUND OF CELLULITE.

YOUR HEALTH CLUB MEMBERSHIP RENEWAL FEE IS $355.00.
$355.00 JUST TO RENEW?!

IT ONLY SEEMS LIKE A LOT WHEN YOU HEAR IT IN ONE LUMP SUM.
REGISTRATION

AMORTIZED OVER THE GRUELING FITNESS REGIMEN YOU ADHERED TO LAST YEAR, THE FEE WOULD COME TO A MERE...

...$177.50 PER VISIT.
CLUB
STAFF

LET'S SEE... YOUR LAST ACTUAL WORKOUT HERE WAS...
AACK! DON'T SAY IT! I DON'T WANT TO HEAR IT!!

AT THAT TIME YOUR WEIGHT WAS...
AACK! DON'T LOOK! DON'T READ IT! DON'T SPEAK IT!!
HEART CHART

AND YOU CURRENTLY ARE...
AACK!! DON'T COME NEAR ME WITH THAT TAPE MEASURE!!!
CHART

HOW QUICKLY THEY GO FROM A JOG OF MEMORY TO A 10K RUN FROM THE TRUTH.

A PERSON'S WEIGHT IS NO LONGER THE MEASURE OF DIET SUCCESS.
RIGHT... REMOVE SHOES... REMOVE LEG WARMERS...
STAFF

WHAT COUNTS IS MUSCLE RATIO! CARDIOVASCULAR CAPACITY! OVERALL FITNESS!
RIGHT... REMOVE WATCH... REMOVE EARRINGS...
FITNESS CENTER

REMOVE BARRETTES... REMOVE TIGHTS... REMOVE NECKLACE ... REMOVE NAIL POLISH....

IN 1987, THE NUMBERS ON THE SCALE MEAN SOMETHING ENTIRELY DIFFERENT!
MY CONTACT LENSES WEIGH THREE POUNDS EACH!
STAFF

"SUDDENLY AWARE THAT TIME AND MEN ARE DISAPPEARING, MANY SINGLE WOMEN ARE CLINGING TO RELATIONSHIPS THEY ALREADY HAVE, WITH A NEW FERVOR TO MAKE THEM WORK."
RECEPTIONIST
"OTHER WOMEN ARE RESPONDING BY MAKING ONE LAST LEAP INTO THE SINGLES SCENE, FRANTICALLY TRYING TO HANG ONTO YOUTH AND/OR GRAB SOMEONE BETTER."
RECEPTIONIST
"FROM THESE TWO EXTREMES COMES STILL A THIRD: THAT RARE BUT PROUD PRODUCT OF THE '80s... THE WOMAN WHO DOES IT ALL."
RECEPTIONIST
MARRY ME, IRVING! AACK! NO. WAIT. I'M NOT READY. WHERE ARE ALL THE MEN? I HAVE TO MEET NEW MEN NO. WAIT. AACK. ICK. IRVING, COME BACK. WAIT. NO. WHERE'S THE PARTY? AACK!
WHERE'S MY CAMERA?

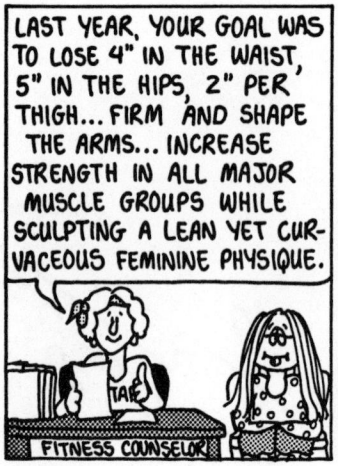
LAST YEAR, YOUR GOAL WAS TO LOSE 4" IN THE WAIST, 5" IN THE HIPS, 2" PER THIGH... FIRM AND SHAPE THE ARMS... INCREASE STRENGTH IN ALL MAJOR MUSCLE GROUPS WHILE SCULPTING A LEAN YET CURVACEOUS FEMININE PHYSIQUE.
FITNESS COUNSELOR

TODAY, ONE YEAR AND $495 LATER, THE ONLY CHANGE IN YOUR BODY IS A MEASLY DROP OF TWO POUNDS.
TAFF
S COUNSELOR

I'M SURE YOU'LL WANT A MOMENT ALONE TO REFLECT ON THIS SOBERING NEWS.
COUNSELOR
STAFF

I LOST TWO POUNDS!!
SELOR

ON MY NEW WEIGHT-LOSS PROGRAM, I RECORD PROTEIN, CARBOHYDRATE AND FAT INTAKE... KEEP A LOG OF EXERCISE ACTIVITY...

COMPUTE CALORIE EXPENDITURE... CHART THE FIGURES OVER TO GOAL-VISUALIZING GRAPHS... CROSS-REFERENCE BEHAVIOR PATTERNS WITH PRIORITY CHECKLISTS.....

WHY DON'T YOU JUST EAT LESS?

IT'S TOO COMPLICATED.

I'VE FINALLY DECIDED. I'LL TAKE THE BLUE ORGANIZER... NO. THE GRAY. NO. THE RED.

NO. THE LARGE GREEN. NO. THE SMALL GREEN WITH THE YELLOW PAPER. NO. THE SMALL YELLOW WITH THE BLUE PAPER. NO. THE BLACK.

THE LARGE BLACK BINDER WITH THE PINK DIVIDERS AND TAN PAPER. NO. WAIT. THE TAN DIVIDERS. NO. THE RED DIVIDERS. NO. THE SMALL BLUE BOOK WITH THE LITTLE GREEN PAPERS. NO. AACK. WAIT. NO. THE BIG GRAY AND NO. THE ORANGE BOOK WITH...

ARE YOU SURE YOU REALLY WANT ONE OF THESE?
YES. IT'S IMPORTANT FOR ME TO LOOK PROFESSIONAL.

THIS TIME MANAGEMENT SYSTEM FEATURES DAILY, WEEKLY AND MONTHLY CALENDARS, QUARTERLY PROJECTION GRAPHS AND A BUSINESS CARD FILE.
VERY NICE.
ORGANIZER
THIS ONE FEATURES SECTIONS FOR FINANCES, STOCK TRACKING, NETWORKING AND GOAL PLANNING, EXPANDABLE TO A 200-CATEGORY DATA BANK.
VERY NICE.
THIS ONE JUST HAS A PLACE TO RECORD YOUR INSECURITIES THAT YOU SPENT ALL YOUR MONEY ON THE WRONG SYSTEM.
SOLD!!
THEY MAY BE SHOPPING FROM THE INTELLECT, BUT THEY'RE STILL BUYING FROM THE HEART.
ORGANIZERS
GUISEWITE

INSIGNIFICANT APPOINTMENTS GET WRITTEN DOWN ON MY HUGE WALL CALENDAR AND CROSS-REFERENCED OVER TO MY NOTE PAD, MEMO REGISTER AND ACTIVITY LOG.
JAN
MEMO
MORE CRITICAL EVENTS GET WRITTEN IN A MORE PRIVATE DESKTOP CALENDAR.... VERY SPECIAL DATES GET WRITTEN IN A TEENSY BOOK IN A SECRET CODE THAT NO ONE CAN READ AND I MAY NEVER REMEMBER.
CALENDAR
THE MOST SPECIAL MOMENTS OF ALL ARE NEVER WRITTEN DOWN IN ANY WAY, JUST TOSSED INTO MY MEMORY.
CALENDAR
THE MORE IMPORTANT SOMETHING IS TO ME, THE BETTER SYSTEM I HAVE OF MAKING SURE I'LL FORGET IT.
GUISEWITE

THIS TRIP I'M ASKING YOU TO TAKE WILL BE A NIGHTMARE, CATHY.
PINKLEY
HYSTERICAL, IRATE CLIENT... PICKY, IDIOTIC MEETINGS... COMATOSE DINNERS...
ONLY A REAL PROFESSIONAL WOULD BE ABLE TO SEE PAST THE SURFACE AND APPRECIATE THE DEEPER BENEFITS OF BREAKING YOUR NECK TO MAKE A HIDEOUS TRIP LIKE THIS.
FLIGHT SEGMENTS!!
MY PROTÉGÉE!!
GUISEWITE

I WAS JUST STARTING TO LOSE WEIGHT AND NOW I HAVE TO GO ON A BUSINESS TRIP, CHARLENE.
HOTELS AND PLANES ALL HAVE FAT-FREE MEAL OPTIONS NOW, CATHY.
RECEPT

I WAS JUST STARTING TO EXERCISE REGULARLY.
MANY HOTELS HAVE FULL GYMS, INDOOR TRACKS, AEROBICS CLASSES...

I WAS ON MY OWN SPECIAL PROGRAM.
YOU CAN EVEN HAVE A VCR PUT IN YOUR ROOM SO YOU CAN DO YOUR OWN WORKOUT TAPE!

BLEAH!!
LOSING SELF-IMPROVEMENT MOMENTUM IS NOTHING NEXT TO LOSING SELF-PITY MOMENTUM.

HAIR SPRAY...
STYLING GEL...
MOUSSE...
CURLERS...
HAIR DRYER...
SHAMPOO...
CONDITIONER...
CLIPS...
BRUSHES...
MAKEUP...
FACE SOAP...
TONER...
NIGHT CREME...
DAY CREME...
EYE CREME...

BOOTS FOR THE BLUE SKIRT...
BOOTS FOR THE TAN SUIT...
BOOTS FOR THE BLACK PANTS...
BOOTS TO WEAR IN CASE IT'S TOO WET OUT TO WEAR BOOTS...
PUMPS FOR THE RED DRESS...
FLATS FOR THE RED DRESS...
FLATS FOR THE BLUE SKIRT...
PUMPS FOR THE TAN SUIT...

ANOTHER MILESTONE IN PACKING...

I'VE FILLED UP TWO SUITCASES AND DIDN'T PUT IN ANY CLOTHES YET.

DID YOU UPGRADE TO FIRST CLASS, CATHY? ALL THE GOOD MEN ARE IN FIRST CLASS!
CHARLENE, THIS IS A BUSINESS TRIP.
TE 72
BOARDING PASSES

ONE FIRST-CLASS TICKET CAN REPLACE MONTHS OF IDIOTIC SINGLES PARTIES.
YOU ACTUALLY THINK SOME PEOPLE PAY EXTRA JUST TO IMPROVE THEIR CHANCES OF SITTING NEXT TO A GREAT GUY??
TO PLANE

I WANT MY MONEY BACK!!

I'VE BEEN GIVING HIM THE EVIL EYE FOR 15 MINUTES, AND HE STILL DOESN'T HAVE MY RENTAL CAR READY.
YAWN.
SPEEDY RENTAL CARS

I'VE TRAVELED QUITE A BIT. MIND IF I GIVE IT A TRY?

GIVE HER THE CAR. GIVE HER THE CAR. GIVE HER THE CAR.
BAM BAM BAM BAM

FOR LOST LUGGAGE, IT'S IN THE EYES. FOR RENTAL CARS, IT'S IN THE WRIST.
SPEEDY RENTAL CAR

I PRE-ORDERED MY RENTAL CAR. YOU SHOULD HAVE EVERYTHING READY.
OUR COMPUTER'S DOWN. NOTHING'S READY.
SPEEDY RENTAL CARS

I WAS SUPPOSED TO HAVE THE SPECIAL $39 RATE.
WHAT $39 RATE?
I ASKED FOR A 2-DOOR.
ALL WE HAVE ARE 4-DOORS.
STICK SHIFT.
AUTOMATIC.
TAPE PLAYER.
AM RADIO.
PHONE.
ZILCH.

I WILL PAY ANY AMOUNT OF MONEY TO GET ANYTHING WITH FOUR WHEELS!!

ONE MOMENT WE'RE STRANGERS. THE NEXT, SHE'S SINGING OUR COMPANY SONG.
SPEEDY RENTAL CARS

I'VE PUSHED FOR YEARS TO EARN THE CHANCE TO HANDLE A BUSINESS TRIP LIKE THIS ON MY OWN.

I'VE CRAWLED...CLIMBED... RUN... I'VE FLOWN ALL OVER THE COUNTRY.

NOW, ON THE BRINK OF PROFESSIONAL TRIUMPH, I'M GOING TO FREEZE TO DEATH STANDING ON THE SIDEWALK OF AN AIRPORT, WAITING FOR A RIDE TO MY RENTAL CAR.

WHEN THEY SAID I COULD GO ALL THE WAY TO THE TOP, NO ONE MENTIONED THE LAST MILE WOULD HAVE TO BE BY SHUTTLE BUS.
SHUTTLE STOP

THIS IS A DIRECTORY OF SHOPS AND THEATERS IN THE AREA.
THANK YOU, BUT I'M JUST IN TOWN TO WORK.

THE HOTEL HAS SEVERAL FINE RESTAURANTS, BARS, AND A FULL GYM.
THANKS, BUT I'LL JUST BE STAYING IN MY ROOM TO WORK.

I MUST HAVE NO DISTRACTIONS...NO CALLS...NO NOISE. JUST PURE, SOLID WORK TIME!
LET US KNOW IF YOU NEED ANYTHING.

MY TELEVISION IS BROKEN!!!

TRAVEL IRON...WRINKLE STEAMER...HAIR DRYER... HOT ROLLERS...NAIL DRYER ...MINI-COFFEE MAKER....
ROOM SERVICE
CHECK OUT TIME

CONTACT LENS STERILIZER... ELECTRIC TOOTHBRUSH...TAPE PLAYER...CLOCK RADIO... CALCULATOR...TYPEWRITER...
ROOM SERVICE

...AND NOW AN OVERWHELMING URGE TO CALL HOME AND SEE IF I'VE GOTTEN ANY MESSAGES.

I DON'T KNOW IF I REALLY CARE ABOUT THE MESSAGES, OR I JUST NEED TO TOUCH BASE WITH THE ONE MACHINE I DIDN'T BRING WITH ME.
CHECK OUT TIME

THIS IS ROOM 922. I MUST HAVE A 6:30 WAKE-UP CALL.
FINE.

PLEASE DON'T PUT MY WAKE-UP CALL ON THE COMPUTER. IT'S CRITICAL THAT I'M UP AT 6:30 AND I DON'T TRUST THE COMPUTER.
6:30. ROOM 922.

I MUST HAVE YOUR WORD THAT A COMPUTER WILL NOT LOSE MY WAKE-UP CALL!!
A COMPUTER WILL NOT LOSE YOUR WAKE-UP CALL.

THAT'S WHAT WE HAVE OUR PEOPLE FOR.
RIP
RIP
RIP
RIP
RIP
RIP
RIP
RIP
HOTEL OPERATOR

HI, IRVING.
OH, HI, CATHY. WHAT'S UP?
UP? NOTHING'S UP. I JUST WANTED TO SAY "HI."
OK... WELL.. ..HI.
IRVING, I COULD CALL A WOMAN WHO WAS A TOTAL STRANGER AND TALK FOR THREE HOURS. WHY DO I ALWAYS NEED A REASON WHEN I CALL YOU ??!!
I THOUGHT YOU JUST WANTED TO SAY HI.
MEN SHOULDN'T BE ALLOWED TO OWN TELEPHONES.

YOUR COFFEE WILL BE UP IN 45 MINUTES.
I COULD GO BUY A COFFEE POT IN 45 MINUTES!
ROOM SERVICE

SARCASM. TWO DEMERITS. YOUR COFFEE WILL BE UP IN 55 MINUTES.
55 MINUTES?!! LET ME SPEAK TO THE MANAGER!!
ROOM SERVICE

CRANKINESS. FOUR DEMERITS. YOU MAY OR MAY NOT EVER SEE YOUR COFFEE.
FINE. WHO NEEDS IT?? I'LL JUST TAKE MY SHOWER AND GO TO THE RESTAURANT!

♪ ROOM SERVICE ♪
Guisewite

CATHY, YOU REMEMBER BOB... YOU HAD DINNER AT THE CHICAGO CONVENTION.
...UM, BOB? ...OF COURSE! BOB!
CATHY? DINNER... ..AH.. YES. YES!

WELL... NICE TO SEE YOU AGAIN.
YOU, TOO... YOU'RE LOOKING GREAT.
THAT WAS QUITE A CONVENTION!
HA, HA! AND WHAT AN EVENING!!

...OH, WAIT! THAT WASN'T THE TWO OF YOU. I DON'T THINK YOU'VE EVER SEEN EACH OTHER BEFORE!!

I DON'T KNOW WHICH IS MORE EMBARRASSING... FORGETTING SOMEONE YOU KNOW OR HAVING A HISTORY WITH SOMEONE YOU NEVER EVEN MET.
Guisewite

IT MUST BE 100° IN THIS ROOM... I'M FALLING ASLEEP ...I'M GOING TO PASS OUT...

NO! I CAN'T PASS OUT!! CONCENTRATE! DIG HEEL INTO FOOT... DIG NAILS INTO LEG... DIG TOE INTO CALF...

...PINCH ARMS... PINCH KNEES... WAD UP SKIRT... CRUSH FOOT WITH OTHER FOOT... JUST A LITTLE LONGER... JUST TWO MORE MINUTES... KICK..KICK.. KICK..

GREAT MEETING, HUH, CATHY?
INVIGORATING...
Guisewite

YOU WERE SO EXCITED TO SEE THE FIGBY FIGURES THIS MORNING, I BROUGHT YOU FIVE YEARS OF PRINTOUTS!
UM...GREAT. I'LL GET STARTED ON THEM ON THE PLANE...

YOUR ENTHUSIASM FOR THE SURVEYS MADE US THINK UP TEN MORE IDEAS FOR YOU TO TACKLE!
AH, YES... WONDERFUL.

HERE ARE ALL THE PEOPLE YOU SAID YOU WANTED TO KEEP IN TOUCH WITH, ALONG WITH THE BIRTHDAYS OF ALL THEIR CHILDREN!
EXCELLENT... EXCELLENT...

HOW LONG MUST I PAY FOR A FEW MOMENTS OF PASSION?

ATTENTION TRAVELERS: FLIGHT 42 HAS BEEN OVERBOOKED. ANYONE WILLING TO GIVE UP HIS SEAT WILL RECEIVE $50 CASH.
GATE 78

ATTENTION TRAVELERS: ANYONE WILLING TO GIVE UP HIS SEAT WILL GET $100 CASH AND A FREE PLANE TICKET TO ANYWHERE WE FLY.
GATE 78

ATTENTION TRAVELERS: ANYONE WILLING TO GIVE UP HIS SEAT WILL GET THE CASH, THE TICKET, HOTEL ACCOMMODATIONS AND DINNER FOR TWO ANYWHERE IN THE WORLD.

HOLD OUT FOR STOCK OPTIONS!!
ATTENTION TRAVELERS: FLIGHT 42 HAS BEEN CANCELED DUE TO LACK OF PASSENGERS.
GATE 78

VALENTINE'S WEEK 1987: SINGLENESS IS OUT. COMMITMENT IS SPREADING LIKE PASTA MACHINES.

ACROSS THE COUNTRY THE LUST FOR "HOT DATES" AND "WILD, EASY FLINGS" IS BEING REPLACED BY THE WARM SECURITY OF MARRIAGE AND MONOGAMY.

PREDICTABLY, THESE THOUSANDS OF NEW BONDS HAVE GIVEN BIRTH TO THOUSANDS OF NEW LITTLE WAILING VOICES...

WHAT HAPPENED?!!
LADIES NIGHT
JOE'S BAR

SINGLENESS IS DEAD, CATHY.
YOU'RE JUST DEPRESSED BECAUSE IT'S VALENTINE'S WEEK, CHARLENE.

SINGLES APARTMENTS ARE TURNING INTO YUPPIE COUPLE CONDOMINIUMS.... SINGLES RESORTS ARE HONEYMOON RETREATS.... I TELL YOU, WE'RE BEING SQUEEZED OUT!

THAT'S NOT TRUE. THERE ARE STILL MILLIONS OF SINGLE PEOPLE OUT HERE LOOKING FOR SOMEONE AFTER WORK.

WHERE'S MY MOM??
CHECK!
THEY'RE JUST SHORTER.
SUSHI BAR -AND- CARE CENTER

HERE'S A GREAT JOKE CARD FOR IRVING, CATHY.
THAT'S WHY YOU AND I ARE STILL SINGLE, CHARLENE. TOO MANY JOKES.

IT'S TIME FOR US TO TAKE A ROMANTIC STAND. TIME TO LAY OUR HEARTS ON THE LINE....

...WHILE KEEPING A SENSE OF COYNESS, OF COURSE. ROMANTIC, BUT NOT TOO INTENSE. SERIOUS, BUT FLIRTATIOUS. LIGHT. YES. COY AND LIGHT.

HERE'S A GREAT JOKE CARD FOR IRVING.
PERFECT.

WHEN CAREER STRESS GOT ME DOWN, I SHOPPED FOR NEW UNDERWEAR TO FEEL MORE FEMININE.

WHEN I LOST TWO POUNDS, I SHOPPED FOR NEW UNDERWEAR... WHEN I FACED FINANCIAL RUIN, I SHOPPED FOR NEW UNDERWEAR...

NOW I'M TRYING TO REKINDLE A ROMANCE THAT I CAREFULLY BUILT ON INTELLECT AND ENLIGHTENMENT. I'M SHOPPING FOR NEW UNDERWEAR.

WE TRAVEL DOWN SO MANY ROADS IN LIFE, BUT SOMEHOW THEY ALL DUMP OUT IN THE LINGERIE DEPARTMENT.

I BOUGHT SULTRY LINGERIE, BUT I'M TOO EMBARRASSED TO WEAR IT.

I BOUGHT A SUGGESTIVE CARD, BUT I'M TOO EMBARRASSED TO SEND IT.... I BOUGHT A PROVOCATIVE GIFT. I'M TOO EMBARRASSED TO GIVE IT.

I THOUGHT OF RENTING A SEXY MOVIE, BUT I'M TOO EMBARRASSED TO GO PICK ONE OUT AND EVEN IF I DID, I'D BE TOO EMBARRASSED TO ADMIT I HAD IT.

I'M BEGINNING TO UNDERSTAND WHY RED IS THE COLOR OF VALENTINE'S DAY.

CANDY, FLOWERS AND A BRACELET FROM IRVING?? WHAT HAPPENED?! WHAT WENT ON??!
OH, IT'S NOTHING SPECIAL, MOM.

WHAT DOES IT MEAN?? WHAT DID HE SAY?? WHAT DID YOU SAY??
IT'S NOTHING, MOM. REALLY.

I GET TO KNOW THAT YOU GOT ALL THIS, BUT I DON'T GET TO KNOW ANYTHING THAT LED UP TO IT ??!
I HAVE TO RUN, NOW.

BEING A MOTHER IS LIKE ONLY GETTING TO READ THE LAST PAGE OF A BOOK.

WE COMPLAIN THAT OUR RELATIONSHIPS GO NOWHERE, BUT DO WE TAKE ANY REAL RESPONSIBILITY ? NO.
NO.
NO.

MOST WOMEN CALL ONLY AFTER IT'S SAFE... INITIATE ONLY WHEN WE'RE SURE WE'RE WELCOME.

WE ATTACK MEN FOR LACK OF COMMITMENT, YET EVERY REAL EMOTIONAL RISK IS STILL UP TO THE MAN.... ANY TIME THERE'S A CHANCE FOR GENUINE HUMILIATION, IT'S THE "MAN'S MOVE" !!

I SEE NO NEED TO CHANGE THAT.
ME EITHER.
WHAT'S FOR LUNCH?

"TO REKINDLE A ROMANCE, SHOW UP AT THE DOOR IN A FLIMSY NEGLIGEE."
HE'D DIE LAUGHING.
"SEND HIM FLOWERS AND POETRY."
HE'LL THINK I CRACKED.
"SING A LOVE BALLAD."
HE'D BE IN HYSTERICS.
COSMO

"BE COY AND MYSTERIOUS."
YES! THAT MIGHT WORK...YES!
COSMO

HI, IRVING. I'M OUT FOR THE EVENNING, AND I DON'T KNOW WHEN I'LL BE BACK!
SAY HI TO CHARLENE.
COSMO

THEY'RE TRICKY WHEN THEY'RE STRANGERS, BUT THEY'RE IMPOSSIBLE ONCE THEY KNOW YOU.
COSMO

CAN YOU DO ALL THIS BY 6:00, CATHY?
NO PROBLEM. I CAN HANDLE ANYTHING TODAY BECAUSE I'VE PLANNED A MAJOR ROMANTIC EVENT WITH IRVING FOR TONIGHT.

I NEED ALL THIS BY 5:30.
NO PROBLEM. A WOMAN ON THE BRINK OF LOVE CAN DO ANYTHING!

I NEED THIS BY 7:00!
I NEED THIS BY NOON!
I NEED THIS BY 1:00!

...CATHY??
WHAT DO YOU WANT?!

I MAKE A LOT OF MONEY AND I GET TO SPEND IT ALL ON MYSELF... I LIVE IN A GREAT PLACE WHERE ALL THE CLOSETS ARE FOR ME... I'M TOTALLY FREE TO COME AND GO...

...AND IF I WANT COMPANY, THERE ARE 32 MILLION SEXUALLY LIBERATED WOMEN OUT THERE LOOKING FOR A GUY!! WHY EXACTLY WOULD I WANT TO MAKE A COMMITMENT??!

AT THE RATE YOU'RE GOING, BY THE TIME YOUR FIRST CHILD SEES YOU, YOU'LL BE COMPLETELY BALD.
AAACK!

...JUST CALL ME A WOMAN WHO KNOWS HOW TO WORK WITH HAIR.

I HAVE TO SAY SOMETHING ABOUT MAKING A COMMITMENT, BUT I DON'T KNOW HOW TO START. I DON'T KNOW WHAT TO SAY.
I CAN'T THINK OF ANYTHING. I CAN'T OPEN MY MOUTH. I CAN'T SPEAK. I HAVE TO SPEAK. SAY SOMETHING. ANYTHING. SPEAK. SPEAK. SPEAK.
WHY DON'T YOU EVER SAY ANYTHING ABOUT MAKING A COMMITMENT??!!
HUH??
THERE! I'VE DONE MY PART...

SURE I CAN'T HELP YOU CARRY THAT IN, CATHY?
YES, IRVING. I'VE WORKED HARD TO EARN MY PROFESSIONAL CREDIBILITY AND DON'T WANT IT TARNISHED BY MORE GOSSIP.
PRODUCT TESTING —INC.—

THE PEOPLE IN THIS OFFICE HAVE ENOUGH TO TALK ABOUT WITHOUT SEEING YOU WALK IN WITH ME AT 8:00 IN THE MORNING!!

HOW DID HE LIKE THE SEQUINED STOCKINGS?!

SEE WHAT I MEAN?

HOW DO I REKINDLE A ROMANCE WITH SOMEONE I'VE BEEN GOING OUT WITH FOR YEARS, CHARLENE?

I COULD BUY NEW CLOTHES, BUT HE WOULDN'T NOTICE... NEW MAKEUP, HE WOULDN'T CARE... NEW PERFUME, HE WOULDN'T LIKE IT... CHAMPAGNE AND FLOWERS, HE WOULDN'T BE AFFECTED...

SOMETIMES THE ONLY WAY TO RECAPTURE A MAN'S INTEREST IS TO IGNORE HIM FOR A WHILE, CATHY.
IGNORE HIM?? OH, I COULDN'T DO THAT.

THERE'D BE NOTHING TO SHOP FOR!!

DID YOU HAVE A GOOD LUNCH?
FANTASTIC! I DID A 40-MINUTE WORKOUT AND A 3-MILE SWIM!

I DICTATED ALL MY CORRESPONDENCE IN THE JACUZZI!
I STUDIED MY FRENCH LANGUAGE TAPES ON THE STATIONARY CYCLE!

I HIT MY HEART RATE TARGET ZONE AND ENDORPHINE PEAK WHILE MEETING WITH MY BROKER ON SIDE-BY-SIDE ROWING MACHINES!

WHATEVER HAPPENED TO THE GOOD OLD DAYS WHEN "HAVING A GOOD LUNCH" MEANT YOU GOT TO EAT SOMETHING?

DO YOU COME HERE OFTEN?
SHHH! CATHY, THAT IS A TOTALLY PASSÉ EXPRESSION!!
Juice Bar

MEN WILL THINK YOU CRAWLED OUT FROM UNDER A ROCK IF YOU SAY THINGS LIKE THAT!
OH, DON'T WORRY ABOUT IT. I'VE BEEN THERE!

Juice Bar

DID YOU GO THERE OFTEN?
Juice Bar

THE TREND TOWARD RELATIONSHIP COMMITMENT IS SPREADING TO ALL PARTS OF LIFE, CATHY.
YOU REALLY THINK SO?

SURE. PEOPLE ARE STARTING TO INVEST IN ONE FINE PIECE OF FURNITURE INSTEAD OF A ROOMFUL OF FADS.... ONE GREAT APPLIANCE INSTEAD OF A SERIES OF CHEAP ONES....

FROM WHO WE DATE TO WHAT WE WEAR, WE'RE LEARNING TO MAKE ONE CAREFUL, QUALITY CHOICE THAT WE CAN STICK WITH FOR LIFE!

MY HEART MAY BE MONOGAMOUS, BUT MY FEET WILL ALWAYS BE FREE.
Shoes

WHEN I GET UP IN THE MORNING, MY BODY IS AT ITS THINNEST, BUT MY FACE LOOKS ITS WORST.

BY EVENING, MY FACE HAS SETTLED INTO PERFECTION, BUT MY BODY IS LUMPY AND FAT.

SOMETIME AROUND 1:45 IN THE AFTERNOON MY HAIR HAS A FIFTEEN-MINUTE RALLY OF TOTAL MANAGEABILITY.

WHEN DO YOU WANT TO GET TOGETHER, CATHY?
WHICH PART OF ME ARE YOU GOING TO BE LOOKING AT?

CATHY'S COMING OVER TO DISCUSS IRVING AND I WANT TO BE PREPARED WITH ONE OF THOSE CLASSIC MOTHERLY ONE-LINERS.

A CLASSIC MOTHERLY ONE-LINER?
YOU KNOW, ONE OF THOSE GREAT POIGNANT ONE-LINERS THAT A MOTHER SAYS AND A DAUGHTER REMEMBERS ALL HER LIFE.

I ASKED IRVING TO LIVE WITH ME, MOM.
AAACK!!

THE CLASSIC MOTHERLY ONE-WORDER.

WHAT HAPPENED? WHERE AM I?
CATHY TOLD YOU SHE ASKED IRVING TO LIVE WITH HER AND YOU PASSED OUT.

SHE WHAT? I WHAT??
HAH! AFTER ALL YOUR SELF-RIGHTEOUS SPEECHES ABOUT LETTING HER LIVE HER OWN LIFE, YOU TOTALLY SHORT-CIRCUITED!

I WAS JUST KIDDING. IT'S FINE WITH ME IF THEY LIVE TOGETHER.
AACK!

WE MAY HAVE LOST CONTROL OF OUR OFFSPRING, BUT WE STILL HAVE EACH OTHER....

EVER SINCE ANDREA AND LUKE GOT MARRIED I'VE DREAMED THAT ONE DAY YOU AND I WOULD SURPRISE THEM WITH THE NEWS THAT WE WERE GOING TO TRY LIVING TOGETHER, IRVING...

JUST IMAGINE...WE COULD ACTUALLY TURN INTO THE KIND OF SANE COUPLE THAT THEY ARE.

I'VE THOUGHT OF A MILLION WAYS TO TELL THEM AND NOW THAT WE'RE HERE....
DING DONG!

WHAT ??!
...WORDS ESCAPE ME.

I WAS NOT THE ONE WHO TOOK THE BEEMER TO THE FULL-SERVICE ISLAND FOR SUPER UNLEADED!
WELL, I WAS NOT THE ONE WHO MIXED #7 COLOMBIAN BEANS WITH #36 JAMAICAN BLUE MOUNTAIN!

WELL, I WAS NOT THE ONE WHO TOLD ZENITH A SLIMY MONSTER LIVES IN THE PC!!
WELL, I WAS NOT THE ONE WHO RAN PLAY-DOH THROUGH THE PASTA MACHINE TO MAKE HER QUIT SCREAMING!!!

UM... ANDREA HAS ALWAYS TOLD ME THAT MARRIAGE GIVES THEM A GREAT NEW SENSE OF RESPONSIBILITY.
OH, IT DOES, CATHY.

IT'S ALL HIS FAULT!!
IT'S ALL HER FAULT!!

IRVING AND I JUST CAME BY TO TELL YOU THAT WE'VE...
JUST A SEC... DOES ZENITH WANT TO SAY HI TO AUNT CATHY??

WE'VE DECIDED TO TRY LIVING TO....
DOES ZENITH NEED A TOY?? DOES ZENITH NEED A NEW DIAPER??

WE, UM...
DOES ZENITH WANT TO NURSE??
THAT DOES IT. I'M OUT OF HERE!

DOES ZENITH KNOW ANY CUTE GUYS?

YOUR DAUGHTER IS GUMMING MY NEW SUEDE BOOTS, ANDREA.
FABULOUS! SHE'S SHOWN SUCH AN EARLY FASCINATION WITH TEXTURES!

SHE HAS A DEATH GRIP ON MY HAIR.
SHE LOVES TO PRACTICE PULL-UPS FROM HER WORKOUT VIDEO!

SHE'S MAKING A SOUND I DIDN'T THINK WAS HUMANLY POSSIBLE.
WE THINK SHE MAY BE PRE-OPERATIC!
EEE-EAAAH

SHE HAS ELIMINATED MY ENTIRE PSYCHOLOGICAL AND BIOLOGICAL URGE TO HAVE A CHILD, IN 25 SECONDS FLAT.
SHE'S VERY QUICK FOR HER AGE!

YOU AND IRVING WERE ABOUT TO MAKE THE BIG COMMITMENT AND YOU LET HIM JUST RUN OUT OF HERE ??
WATCHING YOU AND LUKE SCREAMING SHOOK US BOTH, ANDREA.

I MEAN, AT ANY ONE TIME AT LEAST ONE OF THE PEOPLE IN THE RELATIONSHIP HAS TO BE TOTALLY SURE IT'S WHAT HE WANTS.

I'M READY!!!

TOO LATE, MOM.
YOU HAD TO GO BACK AND CHECK THAT THE COFFEE WAS UNPLUGGED, DIDN'T YOU ??

SAY HI TO AUNT CATHY, ZENITH.
"AUNT CATHY, AUNT CATHY"... THIS IS WHAT YOU'RE DOOMING YOURSELF TO.

A LIFETIME OF OTHER PEOPLE'S CHILDREN CALLING YOU "AUNT CATHY," BUT NO ONE TO CALL YOUR OWN. YOUR FATHER AND I THINK IT'S JUST PATHETIC.

SAY HI TO AUNT GRANDMA, ZENITH.
AUNT GRANDMA ?? AM I YOUR AUNT GRANDMA ??

YOU TRICKED ME.
COME ON IN HERE, UNCLE GRANDPA !!

HERE, ZENITH, CAN AUNT GRANDMA HELP YOU.....
NO. BY LOCATING AN OBJECT OUT OF SIGHT, ZENITH LEARNS THE DUAL LESSON OF OBJECT PERMANENCE AND ABSTRACTION.

HERE. SIT ON MY LAP.
UM... WE LIKE TO USE HER "SIT" TIME TO INCREASE VESTIBULAR COMPETENCY BY PRACTICING LINEAR OR ROTARY MOVEMENTS.

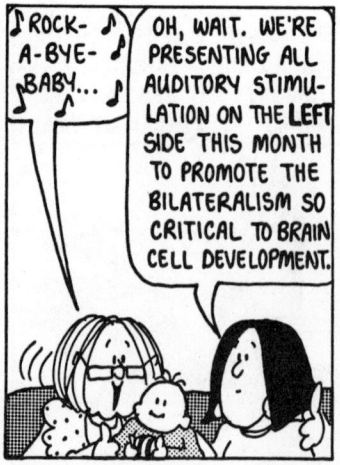
♪ROCK-A-BYE-BABY...♪
OH, WAIT. WE'RE PRESENTING ALL AUDITORY STIMULATION ON THE LEFT SIDE THIS MONTH TO PROMOTE THE BILATERALISM SO CRITICAL TO BRAIN CELL DEVELOPMENT.

I NO LONGER KNOW ANYTHING ABOUT THE ONE SUBJECT I'M AN EXPERT ON.

IRVING, WE'VE BEEN GOING OUT FOR YEARS. MAYBE WE SHOULD, UM... GO LOOK AT CONDOMINIUMS OR SOMETHING.
CONDO-MINIUMS? OH, NO. HOO, BOY, NO! I AM NOT READY FOR CONDO-MINIUMS!!
CLASSIFIED
SPORTS
WELL, MAYBE WE COULD JUST LOOK AT SOME FURNITURE.
OH, NO. NO FURNI-TURE!
UM... LAMPS?
NO LAMPS.
APPLIANCES?
AACK. NO APPLIANCES!
CLASSIFIED
READY TO ORDER?
NO FOOD! NO COOKING! JUST WATER, WATER IN A PAPER CUP TO GO!!
THIS YOUR FIRST DATE?
LET'S JUST SAY HE KNOWS HOW TO KEEP THINGS FRESH....
GWSCHWITZ

I'LL TAKE ZENITH SO YOU TWO CAN TALK.
OK. REMEMBER OUR RESPONSE SEQUENCE FOR FUSSING, HONEY.
WAAH!

1. PLAY THE DVOŘÁK PIANO QUINTET IN "A"...
2. 2-MINUTE SILENT ROCK WITH HEAD PAT...
3. 4-MINUTE "BOUNCY WALK" TO INDIAN HARVEST CHANT..
4. ITALIAN LULLABYE...
WAAH!

NOTHING COMFORTS AN INFANT LIKE HAVING ALL PRIMARY CARE-GIVERS FOLLOW THE SAME FAMILIAR PATTERNS OF SOUND AND TOUCH!

QUIT CRYING AND I'LL GIVE YOU A CAR.
DA!

I THOUGHT YOU WOULD HAVE FOUND ANOTHER JOB AND GONE BACK TO WORK BY NOW, ANDREA.
IT'S SO HARD TO KNOW WHAT TO DO, CATHY...

I MEAN, I THINK I KNOW WHAT'S RIGHT AND THEN I THINK ABOUT THE ENDLESS MEANINGLESS CHORES...

THE HASSLES...THE LOSS OF CONTROL.... DO THE REWARDS REALLY JUSTIFY HAVING EVERY SECOND OF THE DAY DICTATED BY THE MIND OF AN INFANT??

IS THAT A DESCRIPTION OF BEING A MOTHER OR HAVING A CAREER?
LIKE I SAID, IT GETS CONFUSING...

YOU LAUGHED AT HOW I USED TO PAT MY STOMACH AND COACH ZENITH'S LEG KICKS BEFORE SHE WAS BORN, ...BUT VOILÁ! SHE WAS CRAWLING AT FIVE MONTHS!!

WHAT WAS THE BIG RUSH?
OH, CATHY, IT'S HER FIRST HUGE HURDLE OVER FEELING HELPLESS IN LIFE! I COULDN'T WAIT FOR HER TO KNOW SHE HAS ANOTHER CHOICE!

ONCE A WOMAN HAS EXPERIENCED THE THRILL OF MOVING FORWARD BY HER OWN POWER, A WHOLE WORLD OF KNOWLEDGE OPENS UP TO HER!!
YEEHAA

...TODAY WE'RE GOING TO LEARN ABOUT SITTING STILL, HONEY....

IRVING AGREED TO LIVE WITH YOU... THEN RAN SCREAMING FROM LUKE AND ANDREA'S HOUSE...AND YOU HAVEN'T HEARD FROM HIM SINCE??
OH, HE JUST NEEDS TIME TO ADJUST.

THAT'S THE GREAT THING ABOUT MEN OUR AGE... THEY'RE REALLY MELLOWING INTO VERY REASONABLE, PREDICTABLE PEOPLE.

IRVING MAY HAVE RUN OFF A LUNATIC, BUT I KNOW THE NEXT TIME HE WALKS THROUGH THIS DOOR, HE'LL BE..

...A JUNGLE SAFARI GUIDE.

IRVING, WHAT ARE YOU DOING IN DUCK HUNTING BOOTS??
I'VE ALWAYS BEEN FASCINATED WITH DUCK HUNTING.

YOU'VE NEVER EVEN HELD A FLY SWATTER BEFORE.
THIS HAPPENS TO BE MY OUTBACK GEAR.

OUTBACK? WHAT WOULD YOU DO IN THE OUTBACK?
CATHY, THIS IS 1987! GET WITH THE PROGRAM! I'M GOING TO DO WHAT EVERYONE IS DOING !!!

... I'M GOING TO GO SIT IN THE JUNGLE AND WAIT FOR MY HAIR TO GROW OUT.

IRVING, WHAT'S HAPPENED TO YOU??
MEN HAVE HAD IT WITH WIMP CLOTHES, CATHY.

LOOK AT THIS STUFF... EXPEDITION CANVAS PANTS TOUGH ENOUGH TO SURVIVE A ROCK SLIDE... VESTS THAT CAN LUG 100 POUNDS OF GEAR WHILE BLOCKING GALE-FORCE WINDS... FATIGUE SOCKS... STORM FLAPS... GROMMET VENTS... TRAMPING BOOTS...

THIS HAT ALONE CAN WITHSTAND EVERYTHING FROM THE SCORCHING HEAT OF THE AMAZON TO THE FRIGID BLASTS OF THE ANTARCTIC.

OH, FORGET IT. LET'S JUST GO GET SOMETHING TO EAT.
IT'S DRIZZLING OUT.

32 POCKETS IN YOUR VEST... 21 POCKETS IN YOUR SHIRT... 15 POCKETS IN YOUR PANTS... 3 POCKETS IN YOUR BELT... 7 POCKETS IN YOUR BOOTS...
I'M STARTING TO LIKE IT, IRVING.
YOU ARE ??
YOU LOOK LIKE A GIANT PURSE.

THE SHOCK OF REALIZING YOUR SINGLE DAYS WOULD BE OVER IF WE MOVED IN TOGETHER WAS SO BIG THAT YOU RAN OUT AND GOT A WHOLE NEW HAIRDO AND WARDROBE.
WHAT DID YOU THINK? THAT IF YOU CHANGED THE WAY YOU LOOKED THE FUTURE MIGHT NOT RECOGNIZE YOU?? THAT IT WOULD LET YOU JUST SLIDE BY WITHOUT GROWING UP??
I CAN'T BELIEVE IT.
HOW CAN MEN BE SO JUVENILE??

WHERE'S IRVING?
HE TOOK HIS PARATROOPER BAG AND WENT OFF TO HUNT DOWN SOME COFFEE FILTERS IN HIS NEW 4-WHEEL-DRIVE VEHICLE.
HE'S SNAPPED, HUH?
LET'S JUST SAY HE'S HAD A SLIGHT OVERREACTION TO THE IDEA OF LIVING TOGETHER.
WELL, IT'S NORMAL. I MEAN, SAY ALL YOU WANT ABOUT OUR SIMILARITIES, THERE'S ONE KEY DIFFERENCE BETWEEN MEN AND WOMEN THAT WILL NEVER CHANGE...
YEAH...
WHEN MEN RUN FROM A RELATIONSHIP, THEY'RE COWARDS.... WHEN WE RUN, WE'RE TAKING TIME TO GAIN INSIGHT AND PERSPECTIVE!!

BUSH JACKET! FOREIGN LEGION BOOTS! UNDERWATER WALKMAN! STOMACH MACHINE! SUSPENDERS! LAPTOP PC! BUFFALO PLAID! MINOXIDIL! BRAN MUFFINS! AUTO-REVERSE!

MORE WATCHES! I MUST HAVE MORE WATCHES!!
IRVING, YOU'RE THROWING YOUR MONEY AWAY ON EVERY RIDICULOUS FAD THAT COMES ALONG!!

IT'S MY MONEY.
OF COURSE IT'S YOUR MONEY. BUT I'M YOUR GIRLFRIEND... I CARE.. AND I JUST HAVE TO WONDER...

...ARE YOU SAVING ANY TO THROW AWAY ON ME ?....
Guisewite

1982: SPENT IRA CONTRIBUTION ON CLOTHES.
1983: TOLD EVERYONE I OPENED IRA, BUT ACTUALLY GOT TOO CONFUSED AND MISSED THE DEADLINE.
Financial Diary

1984: OPENED IRA. WAS IMMEDIATELY TOLD I'D DONE IT AT THE WRONG PLACE.
1985: MOVED IRA TO A NEW PLACE. WAS IMMEDIATELY TOLD IT WAS THE WRONG NEW PLACE.
Financial Diary

1986: HIRED AN IRA MANAGER. INSTANTLY KNEW I'D PICKED THE WRONG MANAGER WITH THE WRONG PLAN AT THE WRONG PLACE.
1987: NEW TAX LAWS MAKE THE WHOLE VALUE OF ANY IRA QUESTIONABLE.
Financial Diary

ALL I HAVE MORE OF AT THE END OF EACH YEAR ARE WAYS TO FEEL STUPID ABOUT THE SAME $2,000.
Guisewite

TWO WEEKS UNTIL TAX TIME AND THE NATION BRACES FOR A PLUNGE INTO EACH OF OUR OWN LITTLE GUTTERS.

NOT ONLY DO WE HAVE TO SORT THROUGH WHO WE ARE, WHAT WE HAVE AND HOW WE'VE BLOWN IT...

... BUT WE HAVE TO SOMEHOW MAKE SENSE OF A THOUSAND SCRAPS OF PAPER, WHICH, IN MANY CASES, ARE ALL WE HAVE TO SHOW FOR THE FORTUNE WE'VE LET SLIDE THROUGH OUR FINGERS.
CLICK!

BIG DEAL. I DO THAT EVERY TIME I CLEAN MY PURSE.
Guisewite

WHERE'S MY TAX FORM? WHERE'S THE FILE THAT'S SUPPOSED TO HOLD MY W-2 FORM AND INTEREST STATEMENT?

WHERE'S THE MILEAGE LOG I SPECIFICALLY ASKED BE KEPT LAST YEAR?? WHERE'S THE MONTHLY CHECK SUMMARY?

AND WHO'S BEEN STUFFING VISA RECEIPTS IN THE ALUMINUM FOIL DRAWER ??!!
BAM BAM

HOW EMBARRASSING. I'M SURROUNDED BY IDIOTS AND I'M THE ONLY ONE IN THE OFFICE.

EXHAUSTED, DEHYDRATED, THE BODY SCREAMS FOR WATER.
NAH... I THINK I'LL HAVE A CHERRY COLA.
Aerobics Class
REFRESHMEN

NERVES FRAZZLED, BRAIN FRAYED, THE BODY BEGS FOR PURE, NATURAL VITAMINS.
NAH... I FEEL LIKE A DOVE BAR.

A TEENSY BIT DROWSY AT THE THOUGHT OF DOING TAXES, THE EYELIDS DROOP ONCE.
YES! SLEEP!! I MUST NEED SLEEP! IF I'M THIS TIRED AT 8P.M., I NEED SLEEP!!
INCOME TAX INFO.

THE ONLY TIME I EVER LISTEN TO MY BODY IS WHEN IT TELLS ME TO DO SOMETHING I'LL REGRET.

I HAVE TO BUY A BOOK! I HAVE TO BUY A BOOK! I CAN'T POSSIBLY DO MY TAXES UNTIL I BUY A BOOK!!

CATHY, EVERY TIME PEOPLE CAN'T COPE WITH SOMETHING THEY BUY A BOOK. MILLIONS OF PEOPLE SPEND MILLIONS ON BOOKS EACH YEAR JUST TO PROCRASTINATE.

YOU DO NOT HAVE TO BUY A BOOK!
YOU'RE RIGHT.

I HAVE TO WRITE A BOOK!!

A HAND TO HOLD... I GUESS THAT'S ALL ANY OF US REALLY WANTS, IRVING.... JUST A HAND TO HOLD.
THERE YOU GO, CATHY. YOU ALWAYS ROMANTICIZE THINGS PAST THE POINT WHERE A MAN CAN COPE.
I DO NOT.
YOU SAY THESE WEIRD THINGS THAT I CAN'T POSSIBLY RESPOND TO.
I DO NOT.
DO! DO! DO!
NOT! NOT! NOT!
A HAND TO HOLD AND AN OPINION TO REJECT... I GUESS THAT'S ALL ANY OF US REALLY WANTS...
Guisewite

ONE OF THE ONLY TAX BREAKS SINGLES CAN GET IS TO BUY PROPERTY, BUT I JUST HAVEN'T BEEN ABLE TO FACE IT.
I KNOW, CATHY. IT SEEMS SO PERMANENT.

INTELLECTUALLY, I LIKE THE IDEA, BUT EMOTIONALLY I FEAR IT WILL CUT ME OFF FROM ESTABLISHING A "COUPLE" ENVIRONMENT.
IT'S SO SETTLED... SO SELF-SUFFICIENT... SO OLD.

HOW MUCH DO YOU HAVE SAVED UP FOR A DOWN PAYMENT?
$37.00. YOU?

$83.50.
ALSO A PROBLEM...

CERTAINLY WE CAN HELP. I'LL SEND IN OUR TOP TAX ACCOUNTANT.
I'M SINGLE. I HAVE NO DEPENDENTS, NO DEDUCTIONS.
Tissues
TAX PREP HEADQUARTERS

NO PROBLEM. I'LL SEND IN OUR TOP INVESTMENT COUNSELOR.
I HAVE NOTHING TO INVEST.
Tissues

ONCE AGAIN, IT'S TAKEN MY WHOLE INCOME TO MAINTAIN THE APPEARANCE AND LIFE-STYLE EXPECTED OF A WOMAN IN MY POSITION. THE TINY SAVINGS I DO HAVE WILL BE SPENT TO PAY YOU TO TELL ME IT'S HOPELESS.

SEND IN THE GIRL SCOUTS.
COOKIES
Tissues
TAX PREP HEADQUARTERS

I CAN'T JUST LEAVE THOSE TWO LAST COOKIES IN THE ROW. IT LOOKS TOO MESSY.
CHECKS
TAX FORM
GIRL SCOUT COOKIES

SINCE I FINISHED OFF THE LITTLE SECTION ON THE RIGHT, I REALLY SHOULD FINISH OFF THE LITTLE SECTION ON THE LEFT SO THEY'LL MATCH.
GIRL SCOUT COOKIES

OH NO! A BROKEN COOKIE IN THE THIRD SECTION! THE THIRD SECTION MUST BE ELIMINATED!! AND IF THE THIRD SECTION IS ELIMINATED, THE FOURTH MUST GO!!

I JUST ATE THE ONE THING IN MY WHOLE LIFE THAT WAS ORGANIZED.
CHECKS
TAX FORMS
Receipts
Misc Del

IT MAKES ME SICK TO THINK THE MONEY I WORKED SO HARD FOR COULD BE USED TO BUY MORE GUNS FOR THE CONTRAS.
LET'S SEE ...NOPE. WE DON'T HAVE YOU DOWN FOR CONTRA AID.
TAP TAP
IRS INFO.
AND I DO NOT WANT MY TAX MONEY USED FOR NUCLEAR PLANNING OF ANY KIND. NO WEAPONS. NO TESTING.
NOPE. NO NUKES.
TAP
YOUR ENTIRE TAX PAYMENT FOR 1986 WILL BE USED TO BUY REFRESHMENTS FOR THE SPECIAL SQUAD INVESTIGATING THE $10,000 OUR VICE PRESIDENT SPENDS EACH YEAR GIVING OUT PLAYING CARDS ON AIR FORCE TWO.
AAAGH!!
DON'T FEEL BAD. LAST YEAR YOU POPPED FOR THE CARDS.
IRS INFO.
ARE YOUR TAXES REALLY AS COMPLICATED AS ALL THIS, MOM??
THIS? OH, THIS IS NOTHING!
YOUR GRANDMOTHER COULD TURN A COUPLE OF SALES SLIPS INTO A CARTON OF CLIPPINGS!
GRANDPA COULD PARLAY ONE INTEREST STATEMENT INTO A MOUNTAIN OF DOCUMENTATION!
THEIR CANCELED CHECKS ONCE TOOK OVER THE WHOLE GUEST ROOM!!
IT'S JUST A KNACK PEOPLE IN OUR FAMILY HAVE ALWAYS HAD, CATHY.
IF WE CAN'T MAKE MORE OF OUR MONEY, AT LEAST WE MAKE MORE OF OUR MESSES!!
I'M DOOMED.
I WENT THROUGH ALL THE PAPERS AND CLIPPED ARTICLES ON DOING YOUR OWN TAXES, BUT I KNOW YOU DON'T HAVE TIME TO READ THEM, CATHY.
I TAPED FINANCIAL SHOWS, BUT KNOW YOU DON'T HAVE TIME TO WATCH THEM... I TOOK THE AUDIO TRACK OFF THE VIDEO, BUT YOU WON'T HAVE TIME TO LISTEN TO IT.
I TOOK NOTES, BUT YOU WON'T HAVE TIME TO REVIEW THEM. SO, ANYWAY, I JUST WANTED TO LET YOU KNOW I WON'T BE BOTHERING YOU WITH ANY OF THIS.
WAAH!!
GOOD THING I STOPPED BY. YOU SEEM A LITTLE DEPRESSED.

YES, I KNOW THAT IF I'D STARTED IT A YEAR AGO, THE BENEFITS WOULD HAVE BEEN COMPOUNDING DAILY, AND THAT BY WAITING UNTIL THE LAST SECOND I'M ONLY CHEATING MYSELF.
IN

I KNOW THAT EVEN THOUGH IT'S A PAIN TO DO IN THE SHORT TERM, THAT WHEN I'M OLD AND GRAY, IT COULD MAKE A HUGE DIFFERENCE IN THE QUALITY OF MY LIFE.
IN

I PLANNED TO DO IT BEFORE. I PLAN TO DO IT IN THE FUTURE. I JUST DIDN'T DO IT YET, OK ??!!
IN

IRAS: THE DENTAL FLOSS OF THE BANKING INDUSTRY.
IN
Guisewite

MY ASSETS? AH, YES. I'VE INVESTED ALL MY ASSETS IN THE WOMEN'S SHOE INDUSTRY.
HEE, HEE. I INVESTED MINE IN THE DIET SODA INDUSTRY.

I PUT ALL MY MONEY IN THE GROWTH INDUSTRY OF FOAMING HAIR PRODUCTS!
HA, HA! YES! EXCEPT FOR THE FUNDS WE DIVERTED INTO THE CHOCOLATE CHIP COOKIE INDUSTRY!!!

HA, HA! I DUMPED MY WHOLE BONUS IN THE WRINKLE CREME INDUSTRY!!
I DROPPED $300 ALONE IN TEXTURED HOSE!!
HOO, HA! $2,000 IN THE PHONE COMPANY!!

AT LEAST YOU STILL HAVE YOUR SENSE OF HUMOR.
IT'S THE ONE THING WE COULDN'T SPEND.
Guisewite

ATTENTION ALL EMPLOYEES: I KNOW THAT WORKING HERE HAS DESTROYED YOUR HEALTH, RUINED YOUR RELATIONSHIPS, AND WADDED YOUR CAREER ENTHUSIASM INTO LITTLE PILES OF TRASH.

YOU'VE EARNED JUST ENOUGH TO DIG YOURSELVES INTO HOPELESS FINANCIAL CAVERNS AND TODAY, APRIL 15, YOU'VE TOTALLY BOTTOMED OUT. I JUST WANT YOU TO KNOW THAT EVEN THOUGH I DON'T PAY ANY INCOME TAX MYSELF, I UNDERSTAND. I CARE. I'M HERE FOR YOU!

SPLAT!

IT WAS WORTH A SHOT.
RUN FOR YOUR LIFE.
Guisewite

IF THE ONLY WAY I CAN DO BETTER ON MY TAXES NEXT YEAR IS TO BUY A HOUSE, THEN FINE, I'LL LOOK AT HOUSES.
YOU CAN'T, CATHY! WHAT ABOUT IRVING?

I'M SICK OF PUTTING OFF MY WHOLE LIFE WHILE I WAIT FOR SOME GUY, CHARLENE. I DON'T HAVE ANY REAL FURNITURE YET BECAUSE I'VE BEEN WAITING FOR SOME GUY... I HAVE NO DISHES BECAUSE I'VE BEEN WAITING FOR SOME GUY...

I HAVE NO GOOD STEREO EQUIPMENT...NO GOOD PANS...NO NICE TOWELS...NO DECENT LAMPS... NO ART...ZILCH. ZILCH. ZILCH!
YEAH... IT'S A QUESTION EVERY WOMAN COMES TO SOONER OR LATER...

IF I HAVEN'T BOUGHT ANYTHING YET, WHY DON'T I HAVE ANY MONEY ??

YOU'RE REALLY GOING TO BUY A HOUSE, CATHY?
YES I AM, CHARLENE, AND I'M TAKING MY DAD OUT TO LUNCH TO CELEBRATE MY DECISION!

YOUR DAD?
I GUESS IN A WAY I'VE FOLLOWED MORE IN HIS FOOTSTEPS.

I DON'T THINK ANYONE BUT A FATHER WOULD UNDERSTAND WHAT A MOMENT LIKE THIS MEANS !!

HOW MUCH?
$75,000.00

OF COURSE THE PROBLEM WITH A WOMAN BUYING HER OWN HOUSE IS THAT SHE NO LONGER LOOKS MOVE-IN-ABLE, CATHY.
"MOVE-IN-ABLE"?
REAL ESTATE

YES. A WOMAN SHOULD OWN ENOUGH ON HER OWN TO DEMONSTRATE HER TASTE LEVEL AND COPING ABILITY, BUT NEVER SO MUCH THAT SHE DOESN'T LOOK MOVE-IN-ABLE.
REAL ESTATE

I'M SUPPOSED TO BE THIN, GORGEOUS, TONED, TAN, WRINKLE-FREE, SEXY, SUCCESSFUL, AND NOW I'M ALSO SUPPOSED TO LOOK "MOVE-IN-ABLE"??!!
BAM BAM

LET'S JUST SAY YOU SHOULD FIT IN A U-HAUL.
LET'S JUST SAY I'M HOLDING OUT FOR A MOVING VAN.

WELL, HOORAY FOR OUR SECRETARIES. ANYTHING TO ADD, CHARLENE?
YES.
SECRETARIES WEEK
98.5% OF THE SECRETARIES IN THE COUNTRY ARE WOMEN, AND YET THE MEASLY 1.5% WHO ARE MEN MAKE 33% MORE A YEAR THAN WE DO!! WHILE WE SALUTE SECRETARIES THIS WEEK, LET'S ALSO TURN OUR ATTENTION TO THE POLICY-MAKERS WHO HAVE MADE ATROCITIES LIKE THIS A REALITY!!
ANYONE CAN MAKE A TOAST, BUT IT TAKES A WOMAN TO REALLY GET A PARTY GOING.
SECRETARIES WEEK

AS YOUR SECRETARY-RECEPTIONIST, I'M THE FIRST PERSON HERE IN THE MORNING AND THE LAST PERSON TO GO HOME, MR. PINKLEY.
SECRETARIES WEEK
I RUN... I SLAVE... I SHARE EVERY DISASTER... I KNOW MORE ABOUT WHAT GOES ON IN THIS COMPANY THAN ANYONE AND YET I MAKE LESS MONEY THAN THE LOWEST FLUNKY ON THE TOTEM POLE!!
AH, BUT I'M THE ONE WHO CAN'T SLEEP AT NIGHT, CHARLENE.
NO WONDER YOU CAN'T SLEEP AT NIGHT!!
SECRETARIES WEEK

LET'S SEE... PUT, "HAVE A HAPPY SECRETARIES DAY."
..NO, WAIT... MAKE IT, "HAVE A MARVELOUS SECRETARIES DAY".. ..NO, WAIT... "HAVE A GREAT SECRETARIES DAY"....
...NO, WAIT... WAIT... MAKE IT, "HAVE A WONDERFUL SECRETARIES DAY"... NO, WAIT... "..A SUPER.." NO.. WAIT....
Have the Secretaries Day you've always dreamed of.

THE EXOTIC OUTFIT: NO IMPACT.... THE PHONY INTEREST IN SPORTS: NO IMPACT....
THE LONG MEANINGFUL TALKS: NO IMPACT.... THE SILENT TREATMENT: NO IMPACT....
THE $5,000 OF NEW MAKE-UP, PERFUME, JEWELRY AND SELF-HELP MANUALS: NO IMPACT....
THE PROPERLY TIMED PIECE OF STALE PIZZA:
IMPACT.
OH, YOU DOLL! PERFECT! I LOVE YOU!!

WHEN I STARTED HERE AT $10,000 A YEAR, THEY GOT ME A $3,000 TYPEWRITER TO TYPE ON.

THE YEAR THEY COULD ONLY GIVE ME A $200 RAISE, THEY BOUGHT A $200,000 PHONE SYSTEM FOR ME TO OPERATE.

THE YEAR I GOT A $300 RAISE, THEY BOUGHT AN $11,000 COPIER, A $4,000 FAX MACHINE AND A $1,500,000 COMPUTER SYSTEM FOR ME TO USE.

WHY DO I GET THE FEELING I'D BE MORE VALUABLE TO THIS COMPANY IF I CAME WITH A PLUG?

WHAT DID MR. PINKLEY GIVE YOU FOR SECRETARIES WEEK, CHARLENE?
SECRETARIES WEEK

I TOLD HIM NOT TO BOTHER.
YOU TOLD HIM NOT TO BOTHER??

OH, CATHY, WHEN A SECRETARY KNOWS SOMEONE AS WELL AS I KNOW MR. PINKLEY, SHE DOESN'T NEED HIM TO RUN OUT AND BUY LITTLE TRINKETS!

...SHE CAN PHONE IN HER GIFT ORDER AND CHARGE IT TO HIS AMERICAN EXPRESS NUMBER.
SECRETARIES WEEK

IF YOU DON'T LIKE SECRETARIAL PAY, WHY DON'T YOU GET A BETTER JOB, CHARLENE?
ONCE YOU'VE BEEN LABELED AS A SECRETARY, IT'S IMPOSSIBLE TO RISE ABOVE IT WITHOUT GOING TO ANOTHER COMPANY AND LYING ABOUT YOUR PAST.

PLUS, EVEN IN TWO-CAREER HOMES, WOMEN STILL DO 75% OF THE HOUSEWORK AND CHILD CARE, SAPPING US OF BOTH THE TIME AND ENERGY MEN HAVE TO BETTER THEIR LOTS.

WHO CAN ADVANCE WHEN EVERY SECOND OF OUR LIVES IS SPENT JUST TRYING TO KEEP UP WITH OTHER PEOPLE'S BUSYWORK?!
SECRETARIES

GOOD POINT. WHY DON'T YOU RESEARCH THAT ALL OUT, TYPE IT UP AND COLLATE A FEW COPIES FOR MY FILES?
SECRETARIES WEEK

I'M THINKING ABOUT GOING TO A REALTOR AND LOOKING FOR A HOUSE, IRVING.
A HOUSE? GREAT.

REALLY? OF COURSE I'VE DREAMED WE COULD DO THIS TOGETHER, BUT THE SMALLEST MENTION OF COMMITMENT SEEMS TO SEND YOU FARTHER INTO THE JUNGLE.
DON'T BE SILLY.

REALLY?? MAYBE WE COULD JUST DRIVE PAST THE...
NOT TODAY, DARLING. THE HIPPOPOTAMI ARE FEEDING.

TAKE ME.
REALTY
LIVING SPACE SPECIALIST

NO, I'M NOT MARRIED. I'M LOOKING FOR A HOUSE FOR MYSELF.
AH, YES. I UNDERSTAND. YOU GAVE UP.
REALTY
LIVING SPACE SPECIALIST

I GAVE UP??
YOU GAVE UP FINDING A HUSBAND.
LIVING SPACE

I DID NOT "GIVE UP"!
WELL, OF COURSE YOU'LL SAY YOU DIDN'T GIVE UP... BUT SOME TEENSY PART OF YOU IS HERE BECAUSE YOU GAVE UP.

I GIVE UP.
SHE GAVE UP.
REALTY
LIVING SPACE SPECIALIST

SO OFTEN, HAPPINESS IS THE EXTENT TO WHICH WE BALANCE OUR GRANDIOSE EXPECTATIONS WITH REALITY.
NEW LISTINGS
$500,999.99
$400,000.00
$299,000.00

NOWHERE IS THIS AS TRUE AS IN REAL ESTATE, WHERE THE PURCHASE OF YOUR FIRST HOME HITS YOU SMACK IN THE FACE WITH NOT ONLY YOUR LOT IN LIFE, BUT YOUR STREET IN LIFE.
$500,999.99

OF COURSE, A WOMAN WHO'S AS SUCCESSFUL AS YOU OBVIOUSLY ARE MUST BE ABLE TO SPEND ABOUT...

THAT'S IT?!!
...SO OFTEN, HAPPINESS IS THE EXTENT TO WHICH WE BALANCE OUR GRANDIOSE EXPECTATIONS WITH REALITY....

HERE, THIS LOOKS GOOD... "COZY TWO-BEDROOM CHARMER"...
THAT'S THE REAL ESTATE EQUIVALENT OF "BALDING," MOM.
REAL ESTATE

"QUAINT LIVING AREAS..."
"BALDING AND SHORT."
"LOTS OF WARMTH AND POTENTIAL..."
"OVERWEIGHT."
REAL ESTATE

FORGET IT, CATHY. YOU'RE NOT EVEN TRYING.
I JUST KNOW WHAT I WANT, MOM.

I'VE GIVEN UP FINDING A MAN WITH A PORSCHE AND AM LOOKING FOR A HOUSE WITH BLUE EYES.
REAL ESTATE
Guisewite

LAST FALL I SAID, "OF COURSE I CAN SPEND $55 ON A HAIRCUT!"...THEN I RAN TO A PAY PHONE, DISGUISED MY VOICE AND CANCELED MY APPOINTMENT.

LAST WINTER I SAID, "OF COURSE I CAN AFFORD THESE $300 BOOTS!"...THEN I SNEAKED OUT THE DOOR WHEN THE SALESCLERK WENT TO FIND MY SIZE.

TODAY I SAID, "$200,000 FOR A HOUSE? NO PROBLEM!"...THEN I DROVE HOME, LOCKED THE DOOR, AND HAD MY PHONE NUMBER CHANGED.

MY ONLY AREA OF FINANCIAL GROWTH IS IN LYING ABOUT LARGER SUMS OF MONEY.
Guisewite

THIS WOMAN IS MARCHING ACROSS AMERICA ON HER BARE FEET TO RAISE MONEY FOR A CAUSE SHE BELIEVES IN.

THIS WOMAN DRAGGED HERSELF UP FROM THE GUTTER, STARTED A MILLION-DOLLAR BUSINESS AND IS SINGLE-HANDEDLY RAISING 4 KIDS.

I'M TRYING TO GET THROUGH THE AFTERNOON WITHOUT SNEAKING DOWN TO THE VENDING MACHINE AND MICROWAVING A PLASTIC BURRITO.

WELL, YOU'RE WAY AHEAD OF ME, CATHY.
I LOVE MY FRIENDS.

WHY AREN'T YOU TAKING ME TO SEE ANY HOUSES?
YOU'LL HATE ME.
LIVING SPACE SPECIALIST

YOU'LL HATE ME FOR BEING THE ONE TO SHOW YOU THE PUNY HOME YOUR LIFE SAVINGS WILL BUY...YOU'LL HATE THE NEXT REALTOR YOU GO TO FOR CONFIRMING IT...

...BUT BY THE NEXT ONE, YOU'LL HAVE ACCEPTED WHAT YOU CAN AFFORD, WILL LOVE WHAT YOU SEE AND SHE'LL GET THE BIG COMMISSION!!

IF I CAN'T BE SOMEONE'S FIRST LOVE OR SECOND WIFE, AT LEAST--JUST ONCE-LET ME BE SOMEONE'S THIRD REALTOR.

WELL, YOU'VE SEEN THE FIRST HOUSE IN YOUR PRICE RANGE! WHAT DID YOU THINK, CATHY?

THAT HOUSE IS A DUMP.

DINKY, DILAPIDATED ROOMS. GRUNGY NEIGHBORHOOD. HIDEOUS DECOR. IT'S A MISERABLE, CHARACTERLESS, ICKY DUMP THAT IN EVERY WAY IS WORSE THAN THE APARTMENT I'M DESPERATE TO MOVE OUT OF!

BUT YOU WOULD OWN IT!!
AH.

YOU'RE MAKING REAL PROGRESS IN YOUR HOUSE-HUNTING, CATHY.
YOU THINK SO?

TWO DAYS AGO, YOU WOULDN'T HAVE EVEN AGREED TO GO IN A HOUSE THIS SMALL.
YES, WELL, MAYBE I HAVE CHANGED.

AS OUR ATTITUDES MATURE, WE START LOOKING FOR DIFFERENT THINGS IN A HOME!

I WANTED TO SEE IN THEIR CLOSETS.

"MONDAY: ATE HALF A GRAPEFRUIT BEFORE WORK. WAS SELF-RIGHTEOUS AND EFFICIENT."
DIET DIARY
CATHY

"TUESDAY: ATE ONE SLICE OF DRY WHEAT TOAST. WAS PROUD AND POLITE."
DIET DIARY
CATHY

"TODAY: ATE FOUR CHOCOLATE DONUTS. WAS SO CHARGED WITH SELF-DISGUST I STORMED INTO PINKLEY'S OFFICE AND DEMANDED A SALARY REVIEW."

ONE WOMAN'S DOWNFALL IS ANOTHER WOMAN'S POWER BREAKFAST.

WHEN I FIRST MET IRVING, YOU SAID, "KEEP IT LIGHT. KEEP IT COOL. MEN HATE TO BE PUSHED."

TWO YEARS INTO THE RELATIONSHIP YOU SAID, "KEEP IT LIGHT, KEEP IT COOL. MEN HATE TO BE PUSHED."

NOW IRVING AND I ARE ACTUALLY DISCUSSING THE POSSIBILITY OF LIVING TOGETHER, AND YOUR ONLY ADVICE IS, "KEEP IT LIGHT. KEEP IT COOL. MEN HATE TO BE PUSHED"??
WHAT'S WRONG WITH THAT?

WHEN DO I GET TO ACT LIKE I LIKE HIM?!

I THINK I'M AFRAID TO ASK FOR A RAISE BECAUSE GETTING ONE PROBABLY MEANS I COULD HAVE GOTTEN ONE BEFORE IF I'D TRIED, IRVING.

IN A WAY, TO SUCCEED TOMORROW MEANS I'VE FAILED TO BE WHAT I COULD HAVE BEEN FOR THE WHOLE LAST YEAR.

THE ONLY WAY TO FEEL GOOD ABOUT THE LAST YEAR IS IF I GET TURNED DOWN FOR A RAISE, IN WHICH CASE I'LL FEEL LIKE A PAST SUCCESS BUT A CURRENT FAILURE.

WHAT DO YOU THINK?
WHY COULDN'T I HAVE BEEN BORN BEFORE MEN WERE SUPPOSED TO BE SUPPORTIVE?

DARLING, I NEED YOU IN MY LIFE. I CAN'T LIVE ANOTHER SECOND WITHOUT YOU.
POP CORN
YOU ARE THE WORLD TO ME, MY DEAREST BEAUTY. MY PRECIOUS. MY SWEET. OH, SAY YOU'LL BE MINE ALWAYS.
Love Stories
I ADORE YOU. I WORSHIP YOU. I DREAM ONLY OF THE DAY WE'LL BE TOGETHER.
LIVE TOGETHER?...WELL, YEAH, OKAY.. THINK OF ALL THE MONEY WE'D SAVE ON RENT.
NOTHING IN LIFE PREPARES US FOR HOW THOSE SPECIAL WORDS WILL REALLY SOUND.
Groening

READY TO NEGOTIATE YOUR RAISE, CATHY?
YES. I'M WEARING MY POWER OUTFIT AND HAVE PRACTICED MY AUTHORITATIVE WALK.
I'VE COMPILED MY BUSINESS TRIUMPHS FOR THE PAST 12 MONTHS, AND CAN SPEAK WITH COMPLETE CONFIDENCE ABOUT MY JOB PERFORMANCE!
CAN YOU SAY THE AMOUNT YOU'RE ASKING FOR WITHOUT LAUGHING?
CERTAINLY. I WANT FI...HEE HEE ...FIV HEE HOO HEE....
HER PRESENTATION'S READY, BUT SHE'S STILL FIXING HER FACE.
HEE HOO HA HA HOO!!
WOMEN
Guisewite

I'M HAPPY TO DISCUSS YOUR RAISE, CATHY. KNOW WHY? YOU HAVE WHAT I CALL THE "EXECUTIVE ATTITUDE."
PINKLEY

YOU HAVE A REAL KNOWLEDGE OF THE FINANCIAL STRAIN THIS COMPANY'S BEEN UNDER... YOU HAVE THE VISION TO SEE PAST A QUICK CASH FIX TO THE LONG-TERM REWARDS....
PINKLEY

AND YOU HAVE SOMETHING EVEN MORE IMPORTANT...
A LIST OF THE SALARIES OF ALL THE OTHER EMPLOYEES.
PINKLEY

AAACK!!
"ACKERLY, $42,000... ABBOTT, $55,000... BAILEY, $61,000...."
PINKLEY
Guisewite

$5,000. YES. THAT'S WHAT I ASKED FOR. A $5,000 RAISE.
CATHY...CATHY... YOU FORGET! I KNOW YOU!!
PINKLEY

I'VE SEEN YOU CRY ABOUT YOUR BOYFRIEND! I'VE SEEN YOU SNEAK BACK INTO THE CONFERENCE ROOM AND EAT ALL THE DONUTS!...I KNOW YOU'RE NOT THAT TOUGH!!
PINKLEY

I SAW YOU AT THE OFFICE CHRISTMAS PARTY, MR. PINKLEY.
WE'LL RECONVENE TOMORROW.

HOW ARE THE BIG NEGOTIATIONS GOING?
I'M DOWN 32 DONUTS, BUT UP ONE DRUNKEN STUPOR.
PINKLEY
Guisewite

I WANT TO TAKE YOU OUT TONIGHT TO CELEBRATE YOUR COURAGE IN ASKING FOR A RAISE, CATHY.
TONIGHT? ARE YOU KIDDING? I'M WATCHING TV TONIGHT.
CATHY
YOU'D RATHER WATCH TV THAN GO OUT?
IRVING, TONIGHT IS A MAJOR TV LINEUP. I CAN'T BELIEVE YOU'D EVEN THINK OF GOING OUT!
CATHY
I'M OFFENDED THAT YOU KNOW ME SO LITTLE THAT YOU'D EVEN SUGGEST GOING OUT TONIGHT!!
ALL THIS TIME I'VE SPENT TRYING TO FIGURE HER OUT, I SHOULD HAVE JUST BEEN READING TV GUIDE.
THIS IS THE BIGGEST RAISE I'VE EVER GIVEN, CATHY. I BEG YOU TO KEEP IT CONFIDENTIAL.
OF COURSE, MR. PINKLEY.
I CAN'T TELL YOU THE DAMAGE IT WOULD DO IF NEWS OF THIS SPREAD AROUND THE OFFICE.
NEWS WILL NOT SPREAD AROUND THE OFFICE.
HOW MUCH DID SHE GET? HOW MUCH DID SHE GET? HOW MUCH DID SHE GET?
PINKLEY
WE'LL KEEP IT RIGHT HERE IN THIS ROOM.
ATTITUDE IS EVERYTHING IN BUYING A BATHING SUIT. I LOOK JUST FINE.
SWIMWEAR
BIKINIS
NO. I LOOK BEAUTIFUL. I LOOK FANTASTIC!
SWIMWEAR
I AM STUNNING! I AM RAVISHING! I AM A KNOCKOUT!
FITTING ROOMS
...AND WHO ARE YOU??!

HOW COULD I DO THIS TO MYSELF AGAIN??
HOW COULD I HAVE SPENT THE WHOLE YEAR WORRYING ABOUT MY WEIGHT AND STILL LOOK LIKE THIS??
HOW COULD I HAVE ALLOWED SO MANY LAPSES OF WILL-POWER KNOWING BATHING SUIT SEASON WAS THIS CLOSE???
AND WHY IS THERE NOTHING TO EAT IN MY PURSE?!!!
THESE NEW SUITS ARE AMAZING!
SWIMWEAR
YES, AREN'T THEY? OF COURSE, IT'S ONLY NATURAL.
WIMWEAR
THE PAST YEAR HAS BROUGHT QUITE A CHANGE IN HOW WOMEN VIEW THEIR BODIES!
DO YOU HAVE ANY BATHING SUITS WITH SHOULDER PADS?
SWIMWEAR
HOW ARE WE DOING WITH ALL THE BATHING SUITS?
WE'RE DOING JUST FINE.
NEED ANY OTHER SIZES?
NO. I'M FINE. EVERYTHING'S FINE.
FINE. LET ME KNOW IF YOU HAVE ANY QUESTIONS.
HOW LONG DO I HAVE TO STAY IN HERE BEFORE SHE'LL THINK I TRIED MORE THAN ONE OF THEM ON??

IS THIS A BATHING SUIT OR A HEADBAND ?
BATHING SUITS

OH, HA, HA! THAT'S A GOOD ONE! HA, HA, HA!!

HEADBAND.
BATHING SUITS

FIRST PASS THROUGH THE BATHING SUIT DEPARTMENT:
THIS IS ADORABLE! THIS IS FANTASTIC! THIS IS STUNNING!
FITTING ROOM

SECOND PASS THROUGH THE BATHING SUIT DEPARTMENT:
POSSIBLE. MIGHT FIT. SORT OF CUTE.
FITTING ROOM

THIRD PASS THROUGH THE BATHING SUIT DEPARTMENT:
GROSS. HIDEOUS. AN INSULT.
FITTING ROOM

FOURTH PASS THROUGH THE BATHING SUIT DEPARTMENT:
TAKE COVER!!

EVERYONE'S GOING WILD FOR THIS NEW STYLE. IT COMBINES THE BUST-FLATTENING FEATURE OF THE ONE-PIECE SUIT WITH THE SEAT-SQUASHING FEATURE OF THE TWO-PIECE!

SEE ? TOP AND BOTTOM ARE CLEVERLY JOINED AT THE SIDE SO ALL THE FAT THAT GETS SQUISHED OUT OF THE TOP AND BOTTOM WILL BOINK OUT THIS SPACE IN THE MIDDLE.

THIS DRAWS ATTENTION AWAY FROM THE CELLULITE EXPOSED BY THE HIGH-CUT LEGS AND GIVES PEOPLE A WHOLE NEW FOCAL POINT TO GAWK AT!

BLEAH! BLEAH! BLEAH! BLEAH!
SHE WENT WILD FOR IT, TOO.

OF COURSE, FOR HARD-TO-FIT SHAPES, THERE'S ALWAYS THE MATURE SUIT RACK.
OH, NO. NOT THE MATURE SUIT RACK!
Mature Suit Rack

BUILT-IN PLASTIC CUPS... FULL SKIRTS...
I WILL NOT WEAR A SUIT FROM THE MATURE SUIT RACK!

YOU CAN WEAR A YOUNG SUIT AND HAVE EVERYONE SEE YOUR FIGURE PROBLEMS, OR YOU CAN WEAR A MATURE SUIT AND HAVE EVERYONE GUESS EXACTLY WHAT IT IS YOU'RE TRYING TO HIDE!

GOOD CHOICE. THE TRUTH IS BRUTAL, BUT THE IMAGINATION'S EVEN WORSE.

SORRY, BUT I HAVE TO RUN, MOM.
BYE, CATHY!
BYE!

I THINK SHE WAS TRYING TO SAY THINGS ARE FINE.... DAD, WHAT'S YOUR OPINION ON THAT?
I CONCUR. HOWEVER, I NOTICED A LITTLE TENSION IN HER VOICE.

YES. I INTERPRETED THE TENSION AS LACK OF SLEEP.
AH. POSSIBLE. I MAY HAVE DETECTED A YAWN.
BUT THE HURRY. WHAT DO YOU MAKE OF IT?
YES. LET'S EXPLORE THE HURRIED ASPECT....

IT TAKES AN EXPERIENCED TEAM TO TURN A FIVE SECOND MESSAGE INTO AN EVENING OF COMMENTARY.

IT USED TO BE THAT ALL THE WOMEN I KNEW WERE SINGLE AND THEY WERE ALL FRIENDS.
ADDRESS BOOK

THEN SOME OF THEM GOT MARRIED. FINE. I STILL HAD MY SINGLE FRIENDS. SOME HAD CHILDREN. FINE. I STILL HAD MY CHILDLESS SINGLE FRIENDS. SOME STARTED WORKING OUT AND PERFECTING THEMSELVES. FINE. JUST FINE.
RIP RIP
ADDRESS BOOK

NOW I'M SEARCHING FOR A SLIGHTLY OVERWEIGHT, SINGLE, CHILDLESS WOMAN WHO DOESN'T HAVE A DATE AND ISN'T TOO DEPRESSING TO BE AROUND.
RIP
RIP RIP
RIP
RIP RIP

IT'S GETTING HARDER TO FIND A GIRLFRIEND THAN A BOYFRIEND.

JUST A SECOND, IRVING. I JUST WANT TO FIX MY HAIR.
HERE WE GO AGAIN.
WAIT UNTIL YOU FIX YOUR HAIR... WAIT UNTIL YOU FIND YOUR KEYS... WAIT UNTIL YOU CHANGE CLOTHES 10 TIMES... I SPEND HALF OF EACH DATE WAITING FOR YOU!
DID YOU THINK ANY MORE ABOUT OUR LIVING TO-GETHER?
OH, NO. I NEED MORE TIME, CATHY.
HAH! YOU JUST NEED TO MAKE BETTER USE OF THE TIME I ALREADY GIVE YOU!!

DON'T TOUCH ME, IRVING. I'M TOO FAT.
YOU'RE NOT FAT, CATHY.
YES I AM. I'M FAT.
YOU LOOK FINE. YOU LOOK LIKE YOU ALWAYS DO.
BUT I'M NOT REALLY LIKE THIS. THE REAL ME IS THIN! I'M 20 POUNDS THINNER THAN THIS!
THIS IS THE ONLY WAY I'VE EVER KNOWN YOU AND I LIKE YOU!
YOU'VE NEVER EVEN SEEN WHAT I LOOK LIKE YET!!

HOUSE HUNTING IS GOING TO HAVE TO WAIT, CHARLENE. I NEED A VACATION.
WHERE ARE YOU GOING TO GO, CATHY?
OH, JUST OFF BY MYSELF FOR A WEEK.
"JUST OFF"? IRVING ISN'T GOING WITH YOU??
CHARLENE
NO, I JUST NEED A WEEK AWAY FROM THE PRESSURES OF MY JOB AND MY RELATIONSHIP WHERE I CAN SORT OUT MY PRIORITIES AND RELAX. YOU KNOW WHAT I MEAN.
CERTAINLY...
...FAT FARM!!
CHARLENE

DID YOU HAVE TO TELL THE WHOLE OFFICE I'M GOING TO A SPA FOR MY VACATION?
IT TAKES A LOT OF NERVE TO GO TO A FAT FARM. YOU'RE OUR ROLE MODEL.
GREAT. NOW EVERYONE WILL STARE AND GAWK WHEN I GET BACK, EXPECTING SOME HUGE TRANSFORMATION.
YOU HAVEN'T EVEN LEFT AND YOU'RE WORRYING ABOUT HOW PEOPLE WILL LOOK AT YOU WHEN YOU GET BACK??
WHAT DO YOU EXPECT ME TO DO??
YOU SHOULD BE WORRYING ABOUT HOW THEY'LL LOOK AT YOU BEFORE YOU GO.
AACK!

YOU'RE GOING TO A RESORT WITHOUT ME, CATHY??
SHE'S GOING TO A FABULOUS, FUN RESORT!
AHEM ...YES. RESORT.

A RESORT WITH MEN?
MEN EVERYWHERE! MEN, MEN MEN!!
YES. AHEM. MEN.

YOU'LL JUST LOUNGE ON A BEACH ALL WEEK WITH MEN??
NO! I'M REALLY GOING TO AN ALL-WOMEN SPA FOR 7 DAYS OF TOTAL STARVATION AND EXCRUCIATING WORKOUTS!!

MY NEED FOR PITY OVERCAME MY NEED FOR JEALOUSY.
ANOTHER VACATION, WASTED.
Guisewite

FROM THE SECOND I GET OUT OF BED TO TRAVEL TO MY HEALTH SPA VACATION, THE DIET BEGINS!!

....OKAY. THE DIET BEGINS AFTER LEAVING THE HOUSE... ...OKAY. THE DIET BEGINS WHEN I PARK MY CAR AT THE AIRPORT... OKAY. THE DIET BEGINS WHEN THE PLANE LEAVES THE GROUND....

....OKAY. THE DIET BEGINS WHEN THE PLANE LANDS... WHEN THE CAB DOOR CLOSES ...WHEN WE ENTER THE CITY LIMITS...WHEN I WALK INTO THE SPA... WHEN I CHECK INTO MY ROOM.....

ALL THOSE WHO DID NOT GAIN AN EXTRA FIVE POUNDS ON THE TRIP HERE, RAISE YOUR HAND.
WELCOME
SPA
Guisewite

AT "THE LAST RESORT" WE OFFER TWO PROGRAMS: THE "TORTURE SYSTEM", WHERE EVERY MOMENT IS DICTATED BY US...OR THE "HONOR SYSTEM", WHERE YOU APPLY YOUR OWN KEEN SENSE OF DISCIPLINE.
I WANT THE TORTURE SYSTEM.
THE LAST RESORT

NO FREE CHOICES. NO OPTIONS. I WANT THE MOST GRUELING FITNESS PROGRAM YOU CAN DRAG ONE BODY THROUGH IN SEVEN DAYS!!
THE LAST RESORT
COUNSELOR

BRAVO. YOU'RE OFF TO A GREAT START, CATHY.
THE LAST RESORT
LOR

YOUR FIRST DINNER, MA'AM.
I WANT THE HONOR SYSTEM!
SHE GOT MORE THAN I GOT.
Guisewite

THANK YOU, AND MAY I ADD MY PERSONAL WELCOME TO "THE LAST RESORT" HEALTH SPA. IT'S GOOD TO SEE SOME NEW FACES AS WELL AS SOME VERY FAMILIAR ONES.
WELCOME
THE LAST RESORT

YOU'VE BEEN GIVEN SCHEDULES AND HAD A TWO-HOUR LECTURE ON PHYSIOLOGY, KINESIOLOGY, DETOXIFICATION AND NUTRITIONAL DYNAMICS.
WELCOME
THE LAST RESORT

IT'S A LOT TO ABSORB, BUT IF ANYONE HAS ANY QUESTIONS, I'LL BE HAPPY TO ANSWER.
WELCOME

WHO'S BEEN HERE BEFORE AND HOW FAT WERE THEY THE LAST TIME ??!

YEAH!
pant, pant, WHEW!
GREAT! KEEP IT UP!!
STAFF

THE PRE-DAWN FIVE-MILE HIKE IS A GREAT WAY TO WARM UP THE MUSCLES FOR THE DAY OF EXERCISE AHEAD.
STAFF

SHOUTING OPENS THE LUNGS AND OXYGENATES THE WHOLE BLOOD SUPPLY... SO LET'S HEAR IT! LET'S MAKE SOME NOISE!!
YEAH!
GO! GO!
STAFF

TAXI!!

I'M STARVING. I'M IN PAIN.
ONLY TWO MORE HOURS UNTIL SNACK TIME.

I'M EXHAUSTED. I CAN'T GO ON!
ONLY 45 MORE MINUTES UNTIL SNACK TIME.

....YOU MADE IT! SNACK TIME!
POTASSIUM BROTH?? I WORKED FIVE HOURS FOR SIX OUNCES OF POTASSIUM BROTH?

BLEAH!! BLEAH!! BLEAH!!
THERE'S NOTHING SO INSPIRING AS A CLIENT WHO GOES BEYOND THE PRESCRIBED EXERCISES.
STAFF
STAFF

AFTER A DAY OF EXERCISE, YOGA HELPS US QUIETLY REFLECT ON OUR INNER SELVES... ..PICTURE THE BLOOD FLOWING TO YOUR FINGERTIPS... PICTURE YOUR PEACEFUL BRAIN CELLS...
STAFF
PICTURE THE PROGRESS YOU'RE MAKING THAT'S MUCH MORE IMPORTANT THAN JUST NUMBERS ON THE SCALE...
I LOST FOUR INCHES!!
STAFF
YOGA
PICTURE THAT WE'RE ALL STILL SITTING IN THE YOGA ROOM.
WEIGH-IN ROOM
STAFF
FOR THE "WAX WRAP" TREATMENT, YOU NEED TO REMOVE YOUR CLOTHES AND HOP IN THIS TUB.
I BEG YOUR PARDON?
Wrap Tub
REMOVE YOUR CLOTHES AND HOP IN THIS TUB. THEN I'LL POUR WARM WAX OVER YOUR ENTIRE BODY AND WRAP YOU IN SARAN WRAP!
Wax Wrap Tub
YOU WANT ME TO LIE NAKED IN THIS TUB WHILE YOU POUR WAX ON ME AND WRAP ME IN SARAN WRAP??
YES. IT WORKS WONDERS!
DOES IT DISSOLVE THE FAT OR JUST EMBARRASS IT INTO LEAVING?
Wax Wrap Tub
THIS IS MY LUNCH??
THAT'S YOUR 300-CALORIE LUNCH.
STAFF
THIS IS A 300-CALORIE LUNCH??
THAT'S A 300-CALORIE LUNCH.
STAFF
WHEN I MAKE A 300-CALORIE LUNCH, IT'S 25 TIMES MORE FOOD THAN THIS.

I'M DIETING FOR ME. I WANT TO FEEL GOOD ABOUT ME!
EXCELLENT, BETH!
STAFF

I'M DIETING BECAUSE MY BODY IS MY TEMPLE AND I RESPECT IT!
EXCELLENT, KIM!
STAFF

I'M DIETING TO MAKE CHARLENE SICK! TO MAKE ANDREA FEEL FAT! AND SO EVERY MAN I'VE EVER MET WILL HATE HIMSELF FOR HAVING BLOWN HIS BIG CHANCE WITH ME! HA HA!

WE WORK SO MUCH HARDER WHEN WE PUT THE FEELINGS OF OTHERS BEFORE OUR OWN.
STAFF

TWO POUNDS?? I'VE EXERCISED TEN HOURS A DAY ON 800 CALORIES AND I'VE ONLY LOST TWO POUNDS??!
THE LAST RE
WEIGH-IN ROOM
BAM BAM
STAFF

LOSING WEIGHT IS LIKE WAITING FOR SOMEONE TO RETURN A PHONE CALL, CATHY.
THE LAST RES
WEIGH-ROOM
STAFF

ONCE YOU'VE PUT OUT THE EFFORT, SOME PEOPLE RESPOND RIGHT AWAY... SOME WAIT A WEEK... BUT SOME WAIT UNTIL YOU'VE GIVEN UP ALL HOPE AND DONE SOMETHING TOTALLY STUPID FOR REVENGE!
STAFF

I KNEW THAT MEN AND FAT WERE RELATED.
STAFF

I FEEL SO DISCOURAGED.
YOU EXPECTED TO LOSE WEIGHT TOO FAST, CATHY.
THE LAST RESORT
Cycle Room

WEIGHT LOSS CAN NEVER BE INSTANTANEOUS, JUST AS WEIGHT GAIN IS NEVER INSTANTANEOUS.
Cycle Room
BODY DYNAMICS

DO YOU REALIZE HOW LONG IT TOOK YOUR BODY TO GAIN JUST FIVE OF THOSE POUNDS?
TWENTY MINUTES WITH A PACKAGE OF DOVE BARS.
BODY DYNAMICS

...OH. WAIT... I DON'T SEE THAT IN HERE..
I'M SURROUNDED BY AMATEURS.
THE LAST RESORT
Cycle Room
BODY DYNAMICS

ARE YOU SURE YOU DON'T WANT SOME DESSERT, CATHY?
NO... I'LL JUST HAVE A LITTLE TASTE OF YOURS.
SOMETIMES I THINK I'M GETTING TOO COMFORTABLE WITH YOU, IRVING.

DEAR MOM...I'M LYING NAKED IN A VAT OF SEAWEED PASTE, BREATHING THROUGH A PLASTIC STRAW AND LISTENING TO A TAPE OF THE MATING CALL OF THE ARCTIC WALRUS.
The Last Resort

IF THE ROOF COLLAPSES AND I'M CRUSHED IN THIS TUB BY FALLING PLASTER, I WANT YOU TO KNOW I WAS NOT FORCED INTO THIS BY ANY ONE PERSON...I CHOSE TO BE HERE, IN A FRANTIC ATTEMPT TO MEET THE BEAUTY STANDARDS EXPECTED OF A WOMAN IN 1987.

The Last Resort Health Spa

SUE THE WORLD.
The Last Resort Health Spa
Groening

I'LL GIVE YOU $10 FOR THAT RADISH.
THE RADISH IS NOT FOR SALE.
The Last Resort DINING ROOM

YOU'RE NOT EVEN EATING IT.
I'M SAVING IT FOR A SNACK FOR LATER.
YOU'RE SAVING IT FOR A SNACK?
I'M TAKING IT TO MY ROOM AND...

...OH, WHAT'S WRONG WITH ME? I COULDN'T ENJOY IT KNOWING YOU WERE THAT HUNGRY. ...HERE. TAKE MY RADISH. I WANT YOU TO HAVE MY RADISH.
...REALLY?

I'LL GIVE YOU $25 FOR THAT RADISH.
SOLD!
Groening

THINK MUSCLE DEFINITION!

BICEP DEFINITION! TRICEP DEFINITION! QUADRACEP DEFINITION!

NOW TUCK IN THOSE ABDOMINALS, FLEX THOSE PECTORALS, FACE THE MIRROR AND WHAT DO YOU SEE ??!

FAT DEFINITION.
Groening

AS WE LINE UP FOR OUR FINAL WEIGH-IN, LET ME JUST CAUTION YOU THAT IN DIETING, AS IN LIFE, SUCCESS IS SOMETIMES OUR WORST ENEMY.
STAFF

FOR SOME DIETERS, LOSING A LITTLE WEIGHT ONLY MAKES THEM REALIZE THEY COULD HAVE LOST THE WEIGHT YEARS AGO, AND HURLS THEM INTO A WHOLE NEW DEPRESSIVE CYCLE OF SELF-LOATHING AND OVEREATING.
TAP TAP
STAFF

I LOST SEVEN POUNDS!!
STAFF

FOR OTHERS, THIS IS NOT A PROBLEM.
KISS
KISS
KISS
KISS
KISS
STAFF

I CAN'T WAIT FOR MY FRIENDS TO SEE THE NEW ME!
JUST REMEMBER... CRASH DIETING HAS SLOWED OUR BODIES' METABOLISM, SO WE'LL TEND TO REGAIN WEIGHT EVEN FASTER, CATHY.
YOUR BODY

ALSO, ALTHOUGH PART OF WHAT WE LOST WAS MUSCLE, ALL OF WHAT WE'LL RE-GAIN WILL BE FAT...AND SINCE FAT TAKES LESS ENERGY TO SUSTAIN, EVEN A TINY GAIN OF NEW FAT WILL MAKE US GAIN EVEN MORE NEW FAT.
YOUR BODY

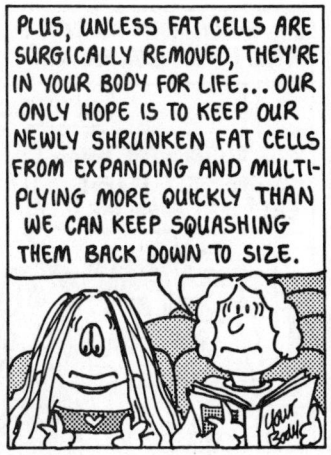
PLUS, UNLESS FAT CELLS ARE SURGICALLY REMOVED, THEY'RE IN YOUR BODY FOR LIFE... OUR ONLY HOPE IS TO KEEP OUR NEWLY SHRUNKEN FAT CELLS FROM EXPANDING AND MULTIPLYING MORE QUICKLY THAN WE CAN KEEP SQUASHING THEM BACK DOWN TO SIZE.
YOUR BODY

CAN'T THIS PLANE GO ANY FASTER??!!
OUR FAT CELLS ARE DIVIDING.
I DIDN'T EVEN SERVE LUNCH YET.
YOUR BODY

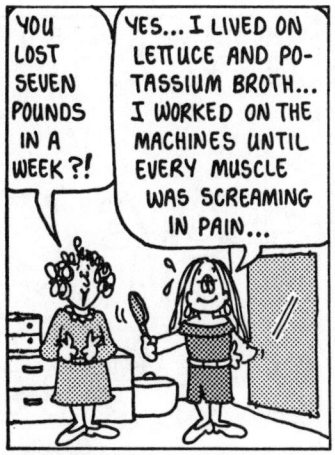
YOU LOST SEVEN POUNDS IN A WEEK?!
YES... I LIVED ON LETTUCE AND POTASSIUM BROTH... I WORKED ON THE MACHINES UNTIL EVERY MUSCLE WAS SCREAMING IN PAIN...

I RAN! SWEATED! CRIED! STARVED!... BUT IT WAS WORTH IT! IT WAS WORTH IT JUST TO HEAR WHAT IRVING SAYS WHEN HE SEES THE NEW ME!!

HI, CATHY. GUESS WHAT? I CUT OUT ONE OF MY EVENING SUNDAES WHILE YOU WERE GONE AND LOST NINE POUNDS!

...AND SHE SAYS WE NEVER HAVE PASSIONATE REUNIONS....

I'M STANDING IN A ROOM WITH A DONUT AND IT'S NOT EVEN BOTHERING ME! I'M CURED!!
COFFEE ROOM RULES:
I CAN SEE THE DONUT... I CAN SMELL THE DONUT... I CAN HOLD THE DONUT... ...NOTHING! HA, HA! I FEEL NOTHING!!
donuts
COFFEE ROOM
GLMBK.
WHAT HAPPENED, CATHY?
I LOOKED TEMPTATION IN THE EYE AND IT JUMPED IN MY MOUTH.

YOU LOOK FANTASTIC, SWEETIE!
MOTHER, I LOST SEVEN POUNDS IN A WEEK.
OH. SORRY. YOU LOOK EMACIATED! YOU LOOK GAUNT!
MOTHER...
YOUR CLOTHES ARE HANGING OFF YOU! PLEASE EAT! EAT SOME PIE!!
I DON'T WANT ANY PIE. I THINK I LOOK GREAT LIKE THIS.
YOU LOOK FANTASTIC, SWEETIE!
THANK YOU!
SHEESH.
IS IT TOO LATE TO START TRYING FOR A SON?

FOR YEARS I BOUGHT CLOTHES IN A SIZE 7 EVEN THOUGH I WORE A SIZE 11. I ALWAYS CONVINCED MYSELF I'D LOSE ENOUGH WEIGHT FOR THE SIZE 7 TO FIT.
...BUT NOW LOOK AT ME!! I ACTUALLY AM A SIZE 7!! NO MORE DELUSIONS! NO MORE BIG PROMISES!
HOURS
I CAN ACTUALLY WALK INTO THIS STORE AND BUY A SIZE 7 THAT FITS ME RIGHT NOW!!
WHAT SIZE DO YOU NEED?
SIZE 5.
Shorts

CATHY, YOU JUST KEEP SAYING THE SAME THINGS OVER AND OVER AND IT'S GETTING NOWHERE!
THAT'S NOT TRUE, IRVING.
THE THINGS I USED TO SAY OVER AND OVER ABOUT OUR RELATIONSHIP WERE CONFUSED AND GARBLED.
BUT WHEN I REPEAT MYSELF NOW, IT'S WITH A CLARITY AND PRECISION YOU'VE NEVER HEARD BEFORE IN YOUR LIFE!!
I USED TO BE A BROKEN RECORD. NOW I'M A BROKEN CD.
Guisewite

I MAY BE SHOPPING FOR A HOUSE, BUT I WILL NEVER SINK INTO SUBURBIA.
REAL ESTATE
I WILL NOT TRADE MY PRINCIPLES FOR A PIECE OF REAL ESTATE... NOR WILL I STUFF THE PASSIONS OF MY ERA AWAY IN CARDBOARD BOXES ONCE I OWN A BASEMENT.
REAL ESTATE
LIKE THE GRAND IDEALISTS OF MY GENERATION, I WILL ALWAYS BELIEVE IN LIVING LIFE ON THE EDGE !!!
EST
...I JUST WANT THE EDGE TO HAVE BLEACHED WOOD FLOORS AND SKYLIGHTS....
REAL ESTATE

THIS CONDO HAS EVERY FEATURE YOU'VE BEEN LOOKING FOR, CATHY.
I WONDER IF MY BOYFRIEND WOULD LIKE IT.
I WONDER IF HE'D LIKE THE STYLE... I WONDER HOW HE FEELS ABOUT CONDOMINIUMS...
10% DOWN
WOULD HE THINK IT'S TOO BIG? TOO SMALL? TOO EXPENSIVE? TOO FAR AWAY? TOO YUPPY? TOO CONDO-Y??
WHY DON'T YOU JUST ASK YOUR BOYFRIEND TO COME LOOK AT IT?
I DON'T WANT TO BE INFLUENCED BY HIS OPINION.
NEW LISTINGS

OF COURSE THE PRICE I QUOTED IS FOR THE BASIC CONDOMINIUM...SOME OF THE FEATURES IN THIS MODEL UNIT WOULD BE EXTRA.
I LOVE THE FIREPLACE!
THE FIREPLACE IS $950 EXTRA.
THE WOOD FLOORS ARE GORGEOUS!
WOOD: $3,000 EXTRA.
AND THE VERTICAL BLINDS!
$1,500 EXTRA.
STOVE? $500 EXTRA.
SINK? $350 EXTRA.
WALLS? $4,000 EXTRA.
DOORS? $2,500 EXTRA.
DOOR KNOBS? $775 EXTRA.
I CAN'T BELIEVE IT! EVERY TIME I FIND SOMETHING I LIKE, I'M UP AGAINST A BRICK WALL!
BRICK WALL: $800 EXTRA.

THAT HOUSE?! NO! ICK!
WHAT DO YOU MEAN, "ICK"? YOU DIDN'T EVEN SEE INSIDE IT YET.
FOR SALE
Realty
REALTOR

I WILL NOT LIVE IN A HOUSE THAT LOOKS LIKE THAT.
WELL, WE DON'T REALLY KNOW UNTIL WE SEE WHAT'S THERE, DO WE??

YES. WE KNOW. AND FOR ONCE IN OUR LIVES, WE WANT TO GET TO REJECT SOMETHING JUST ON LOOKS WITHOUT HAVING TO SEARCH FOR INNER BEAUTY! WE HATE HOW THAT HOUSE LOOKS! HA, HA! BLEAH!! HA, HA!!

YOU HURT ITS FEELINGS.
OH, ICK.

I LOVED THAT HOUSE, MOM!
I LOVED IT TOO, CATHY!
DIDN'T YOU THINK IT WAS A LITTLE SMALL?
YES! TOO SMALL! NO RESALE VALUE!
FOR SALE
Realty

BUT THE SMALLNESS MADE IT COZY.
EVERYONE LOVES A COZY HOUSE!
I THINK MORE PEOPLE LIKE BIG HOUSES.
YES! BIGGER IS ALWAYS BETTER!

MAYBE THAT HOUSE IS TOO BIG FOR ONE PERSON.
YOU'RE RIGHT! TOO BIG!
I THOUGHT YOU THOUGHT IT WAS TOO SMALL.
YES! TOO SMALL! TOO SMALL IN A BIG WAY!

AAAGH!
IN THE SHORT RUN, I'M DRIVING HER CRAZY. IN THE LONG RUN, SHE'LL THINK OF ME AS "SUPPORTIVE."
SALE

WHEN A MAN LETS A WOMAN WATCH SPORTS WITH HIM ON TV, HE'S LETTING HER INTO A SACRED PART OF HIS WORLD.

THIS IS WHAT WE LOVE... WHAT WE LIVE FOR! THE FEARLESS DRIVE... INCREDIBLE STRENGTH.. LASER REACTIONS... BRILLIANT TEAMWORK... FINESSE...

WATCH A MAN'S HEROES UP CLOSE, CATHY, AND YOU'LL SEE EVERYTHING THE MAN IS STRIVING TO BE IN HIS LIFE!

I WANT YOU TO BE MORE LIKE SPUDS McKENZIE!
GO HOME.